119762

P9-ECP-548

LIFE Pacific College
Alumni Library
1100 West Covina Blvd.
San Dimas, CA 91773

The work of Alfred Plummer in the field of New Testament studies has always been recognized and appreciated by the serious Bible student. With the publication of his work on Paul's letter to the Philippians we have available a work which is at once the product of great scholarship, but at the same time of great study value to the layman.

Plummer's concern is to let the message of Philippians speak for itself, often making reference to the original language when greater insight into the meaning of the passage can be gained.

This volume provides an excellent balance between exegesis (what does it say) and exposition (what does it mean) making it a valuable tool for the study of Paul's letter of joy.

A Commentary on St. Paul's Epistle to The Philippians

ALFRED PLUMMER

evangelical
masterworks

FLEMING H. REVELL COMPANY

Old Tappan, New Jersey

ISBN 0-8007-1099-1
Printed in the United States of America

227.6
P736c

LIFE Pacific College
Alumni Library
1100 West Covina Blvd.
San Dimas, CA 91773

L.I.F.E. College Library
1100 Glendale Blvd.
Los Angeles, Calif. 90026

INTRODUCTION

I. PHILIPPI

THE passage of the Gospel from Eastern to Western civilization is an event of the highest importance and interest in the history of the Christian Church. With the exception of the extension of the offer of salvation from Jews to Gentiles, there is hardly anything of greater importance in the progress of Apostolic Christianity. It was an advance from a world in which the best elements of civilization were to be found in Judaism, to a world in which the best elements were centred in the art and literature of Greece, and in the military and political organization of Rome. Divine religion was seeking friendship with human philosophy and human law.

It did not come uninvited. Macedonia, half Greek and half Roman, took the initiative under special guidance from heaven. The Spirit intimated that St. Paul, Silas and Timothy were not to preach the word in Asia, Mysia, or Bithynia : and, when Troas was reached and Luke had joined them, a man of Macedonia appeared to the Apostle with the urgent appeal, ' Come over into Macedonia and help us ' (Acts xvi. 6 ff.). Possibly the first ship that was available after this summons reached him was one that was bound for Neapolis (*Kavalla*), the port of Philippi, about nine or ten miles from it, and separated from it by a ridge which was then called Symbolum, and is about 1600 feet above the sea. More probably St. Paul saw the great advantages of starting from such a centre as Philippi, and chose his ship accordingly.

v

025354

Philippi was founded by Philip of Macedon, father of the great Alexander. Its original name was Crenides (κρηνίδες), from the numerous streams which feed the Gangites or Gangas, the river beside which Lydia and her companions worshipped. B.C. 168 Macedonia was conquered by the Romans, who divided the country into four districts, which were kept rigidly distinct, on the principle of *Divide et impera*. Philippi was in the first of these four districts, which had Amphipolis as its capital. B.C. 149 a different policy was adopted. The whole of Macedonia was united with Epirus to form the Roman Province of Macedonia, with Thessalonica as its capital. But the changes of greatest interest to the Christian historian came a century later. B.C. 42, Roman Imperialism, as represented by Octavian, the future Augustus, and Mark Antony, triumphed over the Roman Republic, as represented by Brutus and Cassius, in the plain between the mountain ranges of Pangaeus and Haemus close to the walls of Philippi. The conquerors refounded the city, placing some of their victorious soldiers there as citizens. After Octavian's victory over Antony and Cleopatra, 2nd Sept. B.C. 31, the city was once more refounded by the victor, and the Roman population was considerably augmented by defeated soldiers from the forces of Antony. It was now a Roman colony with the *Jus Italicum*, which freed it from the tribute usually paid by conquered states to Rome. Thus its inhabitants had all the rights and privileges of Romans, and like other Roman colonies, it became a miniature Rome. The Macedonian inhabitants seem to have become completely Romanized, rejoicing in imitating Rome, and resenting changes which were not Roman (Acts xvi. 21). Their magistrates were called *duumviri*, and were attended by *lictors*, who carried *fasces*. The colonial *duumviri* sometimes assumed the title of ' praetors,' and seem to have done so at Philippi, for St. Luke calls them στρατηγοί; but he leaves us in doubt as to whether these στρατηγοί were the same as the ἄρχοντες before whom the missionaries were first taken by the infuriated mob. His Book of Acts is mainly the history of the passage of the Gospel from Jerusalem to Rome, and he takes pleasure in thinking of Philippi as a leading Roman city at the opening of the new Christian campaign. The story is of a march from a little modern Rome to the great ancient original.* At the present time there are two, if not three, sites to be noted at Philippi. The modern village, *Felibedjik* (Little Philippi, to distinguish it from Philippopoli in Bulgaria) is some distance from the very considerable ruins of the city founded by Augustus ; and it is doubtful whether these ruins occupy the site of the city founded by Philip. Appian says that Philip's city was on a hill,† whereas the ruins of the city which became so dear to St. Paul are in the plain near the river.

There had been two reasons for the position and prosperity of the original Philippi ; the proximity of gold-mines and the fertility of the plain. The mines were exhausted long before St. Paul's time, and the fertility of the neighbourhood, if he knew of it, was not one of the things which attracted him. That the inhabitants were, like himself, Roman citizens was no doubt one of the reasons why he selected it as the first centre for the new mission to Western civilization. Another advantage was that the great *Via Egnatia*, the main high-road between East and West, passed through Philippi, dividing the city into its two main portions. A third point of importance was that there was a Jewish settlement there ; and it was a general principle with the earliest Christian missionaries that the Gospel must be preached first to the Jews (Acts xiii. 46, 47 ; xviii. 6 ; xxviii. 28).

The Jewish settlement was so small that it did not possess

---

* The reading in Acts xvi. 12 is very uncertain. Hort's conjectural suggestion of Πιερίδος for μερίδος has met with very little approval. Whichever reading we adopt, the meaning of πρώτη remains doubtful ; and Blass would change πρώτη to πρώτης. Perhaps ' a city of the first rank,' ' no mean city,' is St. Luke's meaning.

† *Civil Wars*, IV. xiii. 15.

a synagogue, but only a 'place of prayer' (προσευχή), on the bank of the river Gangites ; and here on the Sabbath the four missionaries began their labours.* The worshippers whom they met seem to have been chiefly Gentile women, who, without becoming proselytes, adopted Jewish principles and attended Jewish worship. At any rate the first convert, Lydia, was such a person, and her house became the home of the infant Philippian Church. It was among 'God-fearers,' or "honorary members " of Judaism, that St. Paul found some of his best material in missionary work, and the Jews hated him the more for his success in wresting these "honorary members " from them.

That 'Lydia' is not an ordinary proper name, but a nickname bestowed upon her because she was a Lydian from Thyatira in Lydia, is possible, and Ramsay regards it as "practically certain." But ὀνόματι elsewhere indicates actual proper names (Acts v. 1, 34, viii. 9, ix. 10, 11, 12, 33, 36, x. 1, etc.), whereas ὁ ἐπικαλούμενος or ὁ ἐπικληθείς is used to introduce names that have been substituted for the proper name or added to it (Acts iv. 36, x. 18, xi. 13, xii. 12, 25, xv. 22) ; and Horace shows us that Lydia was a name borne by women who were not Lydians (*Odes* I. viii. 1, III. ix. 6). The Lydian hypothesis is not generally adopted. That Lydia is to be identified with either Euodia or Syntyche is pure conjecture (see on iv. 2). It need not surprise us that she receives no special message and is not mentioned in the Epistle. No greetings to individuals are sent ; and she may have died or have left Philippi before the Epistle was written.

The girl who was possessed by a spirit of divination (lit. 'a spirit, Pytho ') was probably a slave, and she may have been connected with the oracle of the Thracian Dionysus on the adjoining range of Haemus. That she was exploited by a

---

* The reading is again very uncertain. We cannot be sure that worship was *regularly* held here, or that there was a building in which to hold it. Probably open-air services took place every Sabbath and other Jewish holy day. Jews like to have their places of worship near water with a view to ceremonial purifications.

company, to get money for them by uttering oracles and telling fortunes,* is mere hypothesis. 'Her masters' (οἱ κύριοι αὐτῆς) may mean her 'master and mistress,' or a family of brothers and sisters whom she served. Papyri illustrate this use of οἱ κύριοι. She seems to have believed in her own inspiration, and she certainly believed in the inspiration of the missionaries. They, like herself, were 'slaves of the Most High God,' and they delivered a message from Him. But just as our Lord refused the aid of demons when they declared Him to be the Messiah, so His Apostle refused the aid of this spirit of divination, when it declared him and his colleagues to be ministers of salvation. Like his Master, he commanded the unclean spirit to come out. The severe beating and subsequent imprisonment of Paul and Silas, which was the result, is alluded to i. 30. How Timothy and Luke escaped outrage we do not know. If there was any evidence that Luke was a Philippian, this might account for his escape. Why did not Paul and Silas avoid it by declaring themselves at once to be Roman citizens, as they did the next day? Possibly they did utter a protest, but in the uproar the *duumviri* did not hear it. It is also possible that on this occasion they readily accepted the fellowship of Christ's sufferings (iii. 10), and were unwilling to deprive themselves of the opportunity of sharing persecution with Him. Cf. 2 Cor. xi. 25. In either case the conduct of the magistrates at Philippi was in marked contrast to that of almost all Roman officials elsewhere. Whether magistrates or military officers, they usually protected the Apostle from persecution, and treated him with kindness. These Philippian officials, first bullying and then cringing, had probably had no training in the grand traditions of Roman justice.

The gaoler probably believed that the earthquake was the result of the prayers which Paul and Silas had been chanting

* " She belonged to some *masters*, possibly a corporation of priests, who made a good business out of her fortune-telling " (Rackham). " Hired by Philippian citizens " (Smith, *D.B.* art. ' Philippi ').

during the night.* This convinced him that they had a
Divine commission, just as the substance of their preaching
had convinced the oracle-giving slave-girl of the reality of
their inspiration. Both saw in them ministers of salvation
(Acts xvi. 17, 30). Lydia, the slave-girl, and the gaoler,
all of them Gentiles, give us three very different examples
of the population of Philippi, and therefore of the very
different elements with which the missionaries had to deal
in this virgin missionary soil. Lydia and the gaoler show
the early spread of the Gospel to whole households. We are
tempted to see in these three converts types which respectively represent Jewish, Greek, and Roman civilization.
But Lydia was not a Jewess, though she was powerfully
attracted by the Jewish religion. That the slave-girl
was a Greek, and the gaoler a Roman, is not improbable,
but cannot be proved.

The ' we '-section in Acts which began suddenly at Troas
(xvi. 10) comes suddenly to an end with the departure of
Paul and Silas from Philippi (xvi. 17–40), showing that Luke
did not leave Philippi with them. The fact that the duumvirs came to the prison, and personally apologized for their
conduct on the previous day, would tell in favour of the
work of the missionaries, and would gain respect for Luke
and any who worked with him.

Some five years later St. Paul was again in Macedonia,
and doubtless at Philippi (Acts xx. 1). The next year he was
certainly at Philippi (xx. 5, 6), where the ' we '-sections begin
again. Some five or six years later this Epistle was written.
In it there is no direct allusion to intermediate visits ; but
the general tone of interest, intimacy, and affection is in
harmony with such facts, and it is possible that ' many
times used to tell ' (iii. 18) refers to what was said at a second
or third visit.

Ignatius passed through Philippi on his way to be mar-
tyred at Rome, and a little later Polycarp wrote to the

* Προσευχόμενοι ὕμνουν may refer to liturgical usage ; but
ὑμνοῦν may mean no more than repetition. So often in Plato ;
cf. Soph. *Ajax*, 292.

Philippians a letter in which he alludes to our Epistle, and possibly to more than one, from the Apostle to the Philippians. After that our knowledge of the Philippian Church is almost a blank. " Born into the world with the brightest promise, the Church of Philippi has lived without a history and perished without a memorial " (Lightfoot).

II. AUTHENTICITY AND INTEGRITY

The *genuineness* of the Epistle to the Philippians is now so generally admitted even by scholars who are hyper-critical in other directions, that one might be justified in assuming it without discussion as certain. Answering objections is slaying the slain, a process which is all the more superfluous, because in some cases it is an objector who convincingly replies to the arguments which a previous assailant of the Epistle has used. Thus Holsten demolishes the criticisms of Baur, only to have his own criticisms similarly treated by later writers. Schürer regards them as more like slips of the pen than serious arguments, and Paul Ewald pulverizes them in detail. Sometimes the words of the letter are misinterpreted, in order to make out a case against it ; sometimes historical situations are invented, in order to show that the letter must have been written after the death of the Apostle. Arguments are used which " are really so weak, that we can hardly believe that the objector could have attached any importance to them himself " (Bleek). " The objections raised by a few hyper-critics are not worthy of serious refutation " (P. Schaff).

The *internal evidence* is of the strongest. It would be difficult to point to any four consecutive chapters in the N.T. as more intensely Pauline. " The tone is Pauline beyond the possibility of imitation " (Jülicher) ; and it is so in so many different ways. Assuming, however, that any primitive writer was capable of imitating thus minutely the Apostle's mental and moral characteristics, it is impossible to find any adequate motive for such a forgery. *Non cuivis Paulinum pectus effingere*, says Bengel ; and if so consummate an artist had existed, would he have produced such a simple, affectionate, grateful, and undogmatic letter as this ?

The *external evidence* is hardly less conclusive. There is little doubt that Clement of Rome (A.D. 95) knew this Epistle. No one passage in his letter can be called a quotation ; but the cumulative effect of the various expressions which may be echoes of Philippians is almost stringent ; so many resemblances can hardly be accidental. Ignatius seems to have known it. Polycarp certainly did. From A.D. 175 onwards testimonies to it become abundant.

Among foreign scholars of high rank the following accept it as genuine ; Bleek, B. Brückner, W. Brückner, Clemen, De Wette, Ernesti, P. Ewald, Godet, Grimm, Harnack, E. Haupt, Hilgenfeld, Holtzmann, Jülicher, Klöpper, Lipsius, Lueken, Lünemann, Mangold, Pfleiderer, Renan, Resch, Reuss, Sabatier, Schenkel, P. W. Schmidt, Schürer, B. Weiss, Zahn.*

The same may be said with regard to its *integrity*. It was probably not all dictated at one sitting ; and at iii. 1 there may have been some disturbing interruption. But that we really have two letters joined together at this point, either of which may have been written first, is an hypothesis which solves no difficulties, and which has little evidence to support it ; for the possibility that St. Paul wrote more than one letter to the Philippians is no evidence that in this Epistle we have two letters dovetailed. Yet this gratuitous suggestion is better than the wild theory that fragments of two genuine letters lie scattered about through all four chapters. There is no reasonable doubt that all four chapters were written as parts of one and the same letter, and in the order in which we have them.

---

* " The attempts made during the nineteenth century to disprove the Pauline authorship now possess merely an historic interest " (Moffat). See also C. R. Gregory, *Canon and Text of N.T.* pp. 205 f., and R. J. Knowling, *Testimony of St. Paul to Christ*, pp. iii f.

III. PLACE AND DATE

Here again we are on firm ground. Almost every indication in the letter itself points to one place only, viz. *Rome*. The hypothesis suggested by some modern critics, that it was written during the imprisonment at *Caesarea*, will not bear investigation. In i. 13 and iv. 22 we have what almost amounts to proof in favour of Rome, and what the Apostle tells us about his own surroundings harmonizes with this. His hope of being released and coming soon to visit Philippi (i. 25, ii. 24) is fatal to the view of Caesarea. Cessation of the imprisonment at Caesarea would mean transfer to Rome.

But during the last few years some scholars, including B. W. Bacon, Deissmann, and Kirsopp Lake, have suggested *Ephesus* as the place from which the letter was written. The theory is less incredible than that which advocates Caesarea, but it fails altogether when weighed against the almost universally accepted view that the letter was written during the two years' imprisonment at Rome. The Ephesus theory is based upon a number of more or less probable conjectures ; the accepted view is based upon well-ascertained facts. (1) We do not know that St. Paul was ever imprisoned at Ephesus. We know that he was imprisoned for two years at Rome, and the letter implies an imprisonment of many months' duration. It is true that 2 Cor. xi. 23 and Clem. Rom. *Cor.* vi. show that the Apostle was thrown into prison more often than the occasions mentioned in Acts, and one of these additional imprisonments may have been at Ephesus. But it is very improbable that there was an imprisonment of many months at Ephesus. St. Luke's silence respecting such an event would be extraordinary. (2) 'I fought with beasts at Ephesus' is supposed to imply imprisonment and sentence of death, a death from which, in some strange way, the Apostle escaped. But it is incredible that a Roman citizen was sentenced to fight with wild beasts in the arena. The phrase is a metaphor for conflict with brutal men. (3)

There may have been a *praetorium* of some kind at Ephesus. We know that there was one at Rome. (4) There were persons at Ephesus related to the Imperial court who might be said to be ' of the household of Caesar.' We know that ' the household of Caesar ' was a well-known institution at Rome. (5) Many scholars hold that Rom. xvi. really belongs to a letter addressed to Ephesus, and in Rom. xvi. 7 Andronicus and Junias are called ' my fellow-prisoners,' and they were probably imprisoned with him at Ephesus. But it is far from certain that Rom. xvi. was originally addressed to Ephesus ; many scholars regard the theory as untenable ; and ' my fellow-prisoners ' need not mean more than that ' they, like myself, have suffered imprisonment.' (6) At Ephesus there is a fort called " St. Paul's Prison." It is certain that the Apostle was never imprisoned in it.

The *Date* of the letter, like all other dates in the life of St. Paul, cannot be determined with exactness. It was probably in the spring of A.D. 50 that he first visited Philippi. About A.D. 55 he was probably again there, and in the following year he was certainly there. Then comes his arrest at Jerusalem, the imprisonment at Caesarea, and the two years' imprisonment at Rome, near the end of which he wrote this Epistle, about A.D. 60–62. Perhaps A.D. 61 is right, about ten years later than 1 Thessalonians. Some put the dates one or two years later, and a few prefer one or two years earlier.

But, whatever the year may be, the letter was written late in the two years at Rome. His imprisonment has had time to produce momentous effects (i. 12–18) ; he is expecting to be released before long (i. 25, ii. 24) ; the Philippians have had time to hear of his necessities and, after considerable delay (iv. 10), to send Epaphroditus, to hear of his arrival in Rome and serious illness there, and to let him know of their anxiety about him (ii. 24–27). Moreover, St. Luke has evidently left the Apostle (ii. 21, iv. 22 ; cf. Col. iv. 14).

We have no means of knowing whether St. Paul's condition had been affected by two events, either of which might have made his imprisonment more stringent, and his prospect of acquittal less. 1. The Praetorian Prefect Burrhus, an upright man, who had treated St. Paul humanely, died, and one of his successors was the infamous Tigellinus. 2. Nero married Poppaea, who was a Jewish proselyte, and would be likely to support the Apostle's Jewish prosecutors. Our Epistle was probably written before either of these events took place. No trace of them, therefore, can be looked for in it. See Lewin, *Fasti Sacri*, p. 326.

IV. OCCASION

We may be sure that during the five years between the Apostle's first and second visits to Philippi there were communications between him and his converts. He would not have remained silent, and we know that on several occasions they sent supplies to him, and no doubt were among the Macedonians who were so generous in contributing to the fund for the relief of the poor Christians at Jerusalem (2 Cor. viii. 1–5). As Philippi was on the great highway between Asia Minor and much of Europe, opportunities of sending messages or letters would be considerable. That St. Paul had previously written to the Philippians is more than we know ; but there is no improbability in the supposition, and τὰ αὐτά in iii. 1 is regarded by some as an allusion to a former letter. On the other side, the Philippians may have sent a letter along with one or more of their contributions. In the present Epistle there are possible allusions to a letter sent by them after the arrival of Epaphroditus in Rome. They may have inquired about the Apostle's progress and prospects (i. 12 f.), told him that they prayed for him (i. 19), wondered whether they would ever see him again (i. 24, 25, ii. 24), inquired about the illness of Epaphroditus (ii. 26), and expressed regret that the money had not been sent to the Apostle sooner (iv. 10). Every one of these features in the Epistle would be quite natural, if no such letter had been sent from Philippi, and therefore all of them put together do not amount to evidence that the Apostle is answering a letter. All that can safely be said is that, if such a letter was sent, our Epistle is to some extent an answer to it. The hypothesis of a Philippian letter sent after Epaphroditus reached Rome does not help us to understand anything in the Epistle ; it merely agrees very well with certain features in it. The Apostle was sympathetic enough to have suspected that the Philippians were disturbed about the delay in sending help, and about the course of events in Rome, and resolved to reassure them. This, then, was one reason for writing.

In addition to this, there was Epaphroditus, about whose illness they were so anxious, now restored to bodily health, but home-sick, who would gladly carry a letter to Philippi.

And, if the Philippians were anxious about the Apostle, he also was anxious about them. On the whole, he could rejoice greatly at their spiritual condition (i. 3–6, ii. 12) ; but there was a want of Christian unity, and a tendency to unchristian despondency and gloom. He must exhort them to be more united (i. 9, ii. 2–17, iii. 16, iv. 2, 3, 9), and must encourage them to rejoice without ceasing (ii. 18, 28, iv. 4). He also knew that they were suffering persecution (i. 30), and would urge them to stand fast (iv. 1). Moreover, he was anxious about grave evils, which existed elsewhere in Christian Churches, and which might find their way to Philippi. He therefore warns them earnestly against the Judaizers who wanted to enslave Christians under the Law (iii. 2–11), and against Antinomians who taught that Christian liberty meant Gentile laxity about sin (iii. 17–21).

The immediate occasion of the Epistle was the eagerness of Epaphroditus to return home.

V. CHARACTERISTICS AND CONTENTS

The Epistle to the Philippians has received a number of descriptive epithets. It has been called " the Epistle of Joy," " the Epistle of Love," " the Epistle of Humility," " the most beautiful of all the Pauline Epistles," " the most

affectionate," "the happiest," "the noblest reflexion of St.
Paul's personal character and spiritual illumination," "the
most attractive picture in the N.T. of Christian life and a
Christian Church," "the love-letter" among the Pauline
Epistles, "the testament of the Apostle and the most
epistolary of all Epistles" (*der brieflichste aller Briefe*).
Let us begin with the last of these descriptions; "it is the
most letter-like of all letters." In other words, it is a real
letter, and not a treatise, or an essay, or a homily, or anything else, dressed up to look like a letter. It is one of the
significant indications of Van Manen's incompetence as a
critic that he can pronounce it to be "not really a letter,
but an edifying composition in the form of a letter." Its
simplicity and artlessness are conspicuous all through as the
natural outpouring of a very affectionate, cheerful, and
grateful, but somewhat anxious and sensitive friend and
teacher, to disciples who (as he knows) admire and love
him, but are in need of both encouragement and warning.
Indications of mutual affection abound (i. 7–9, 25, 26, ii. 2,
12, 17, 18, 28, iii. 16, iv. 1, 14–17). The topics come one
after another in a manner which is natural enough, but
which shows no very careful plan; and the letter is therefore
delightfully informal, but somewhat difficult to analyse.
Here and there, as in the great doctrinal passage (ii. 6–11),
and in personal explanations (iii. 4–12, iv. 11–13), the wording seems to have been prepared with some care beforehand.
But, for the most part, the Apostle has simply made up his
mind as to the subjects which he will talk about, and he
utters them as they occur to his memory. *Talk* about them
is exactly what he does. The most perfect kind of letter-
writing is that which comes nearest to good conversation;
and of all the Pauline Epistles none comes nearer to that
than the letter before us. As one might expect in what is
addressed by a loving master to loving and dutiful pupils,
the letter simply swings backwards and forwards between
what concerns them, and therefore greatly interests him, and
what concerns him, and is sure to interest them. Both of
these elements are a self-revelation of the writer. They tell

B

us of his prison-thoughts ;—his joys and his sorrows and the source of his strength in combining joy and sorrow with regard to the chequered present and the uncertain future.

The alternations between those whom he addresses and himself are roughly as follows : i. 3–11 Thanksgiving and Prayer for the Philippians ; i. 12–26 Personal Information about the Apostle ; i. 27–ii. 18 Exhortation and Counsel to the Philippians ; ii. 19–iii. 1 Personal Information about the Apostle ; iii. 2–iv. 9 Warnings and Exhortations to the Philippians ; iv. 10–20 The Apostle's Gratitude for their affectionate Gift.

There is no hint, not even in ii. 6–11 or iii. 2–19, that the Philippians needed correction in matters of doctrine ; ii. 6–11 is part of an exhortation with regard to conduct, and iii. 2–19 is a warning against evils of doctrine and practice which exist elsewhere and might become rife at Philippi.

As already stated, the absence of a prearranged plan makes the letter difficult to analyse. But the following scheme may be of some help towards a connected view of its contents.

VI. THE EPISTLES TO THE MACEDONIAN CHURCHES

The Epistle to the Philippians closes the little group of letters which St. Paul addressed to the Churches of Macedonia, a group of intense interest for the student of the work and character of St. Paul. These three Epistles are an imperishable memorial of his labour and method in founding, cherishing and educating these Churches : and that work was one of the most momentous ventures in his courageous experiments for the furtherance of the Gospel. The Epistles are only a portion, and perhaps a small portion, of the intercourse, literary and oral, which passed between the Apostle of the Gentiles and the congregations who were his first and most beloved converts on European soil. It is highly instructive to study the three Epistles together and to notice the characteristics which they have in common : and it is hoped that commentaries on each of them, similar in plan and in the amount of explanation offered, will contribute something to such study. Although ten years of a very active and very varied life lie between 1 Thessalonians and Philippians, yet the resemblance in tone is remarkable, especially as regards the mutual affection between the Apostle and his converts. Neither to the

Thessalonians nor to the Philippians does he use his official title of Apostle. They have never resisted his authority and he has no need to remind them of it. In all three letters he thanks God for the converts' steadfastness and progress. He can say of both Thessalonians (i. Thess. ii. 19) and Philippians (iv. 1) that they are his crown and his joy, his joy in this life and a crown that will do him honour in the life to come. He is as sure of their love for him as of his own for them ; and he is willing to part with his beloved and most helpful Timothy in order to serve either of them (1 Thess. iii. 2 ; Phil. ii. 19). He prays for them, and he counts on their prayers for himself. Both he and they know what it is to suffer persecution, and therefore can not only feel sympathy for one another, but share in the same kind of suffering.

Apart from the spiritual welfare of his converts there were few objects which he had more at heart than the fund for the succour of the poor Christians in Judaea, the Palestine Relief Fund ; and in supporting this his dear Macedonians had done excellently. He says to the Corinthians, ' Let me make known to you, my Brothers, the grace of God which has been and still is being exhibited very remarkably in the Churches of Macedonia. In the midst of an ordeal of affliction which has served to bring out their genuine Christianity, their overflowing happiness, combined with quite desperate poverty, has issued in a rich stream of simpleminded generosity. For I can testify that up to the very limits, yes, and beyond the limits of their very slender means, they have given freely, and this without one word of suggestion from me. So far from my asking them for help, they begged us most urgently to be allowed the privilege of taking part in the work of ministering to the necessities of their fellow-Christians in Jerusalem. I should be misleading you if I were to say that in this they acted just as we expected that they would ; one does not expect very much from very poor people ; they did far more than we expected. It was their own selves that they gave first and foremost to the Lord and also to us, and they made

the offering in both cases because it was so willed by God '
(2 Cor. viii. 1 f.).

This generous commendation of the Macedonians to
another Church is quite in harmony with the expressions
which he uses respecting them in the letters addressed
to themselves.

VII. COMMENTARIES

Only a selection is given here. A similar list with
descriptive notes on the various commentaries will be
found in the excellent volume on the Epistle in the International Critical Commentary by Dr. Marvin R. Vincent,
who has had the advantage of coming late (1897) in a very
distinguished series of commentators. In the following
summary foreign works which have been translated into
English are inserted in the English list.

ON THE GREEK TEXT.

Patristic.

Greek. Chrysostom, Theodore of Mopsuestia,* Theodoret,
Oecumenius, Theophylact.
Latin. Ambrosiaster, Pelagius.

Reformers.

Erasmus, Zwingli, Beza, Calvin, Musculus.

Modern.

Bengel, *Gnomon Novi Testamenti,* 1742 ; tr. 1857, 1860.
Neander, tr. 1851.
Webster and Wilkinson, 1855–1861.

---

* Swete's admirable edition of the Latin Version with the Greek
fragments has been often used for the notes in this volume. For
information respecting all these writers see Swete's *Patristic Study,*
and Hastings, *D.B.* vol. V. art. ' Patristic Commentaries ' by
C. H. Turner.

Alford, 1857, 5th ed. 1871.
Olshausen, 1830 ; tr. 1858.
C. Wordsworth, 1859.
Meyer, 4th ed. tr. 1875.
Eadie, 1877, 2nd ed. 1884.
Ellicott, 2nd ed. 1861, 5th ed. 1888.
Lightfoot, 6th ed. 1891.
C. J. Vaughan, 1885.
J. Agar Beet, 1890.
Moule (*Cambridge Greek Testament*), 1897.
B. Weiss, 1902 ; tr. 1906.
Kennedy (*Expositor's Greek Testament*), 1903.

On the English Versions.

A. Barry (*Ellicott's Commentary*), 1879.
Gwynn (*Speaker's Commentary*), 1881.
Lumby (*Schaff's Commentary*), 1882.
G. C. Martin (*Century Bible*).
Sadler, 1889.
Drummond (*International Handbooks*), 1899.
R. R. Smith, *The Epistle of St. Paul's First Trial*, 1899.
Rainy (*Expositor's Bible*).
Strachan (*Westminster New Testament*), 1910.
Maurice Jones (*Westminster Commentaries*), 1917.
A. T. Robertson, *Paul's Joy in Christ*, 1918.

New Translations in English.

The Twentieth Century New Testament, 1900.
Weymouth, *The N.T. in Modern Speech*, 1905.
Way, *The Letters of St. Paul*, 2nd ed. 1906.
Moffat, *The N.T., a New Translation*, 1913.
Cunnington, *The New Covenant*, 1914.

There are valuable articles on the Epistle in Smith's
DB. by W. T. Bullock ; Hastings' *DB.* by J. Gibb ; Hastings'
DAC. by D. Mackensie ; *Encyclopaedia Britannica*, 11th ed.,
by Moffatt ; Murray's *Illustr. BD.* by Moule.

See also the article on ' Paul ' in Hastings' *DCG*. II. by Sanday.

The literature on the great doctrinal passage ii. 5–11, especially with regard to the Kenosis, is considerable ; *e.g.* Godet on Jn. i. 14, 1879 ; Westcott on Jn. i. 14, 1880. Hutton, *Theological Essays*, 1881, 1888, Essay vii. Bruce, *Humiliation of Christ*, 1889. Fairbairn, *Christ in Modern Theology*, 1893. Bright, *Waymarks in Church History*, 1894. Gore, *Dissertations*, 1895. Mason, *Conditions of our Lord's Life on Earth*, 1896. Powell, *Principle of the Incarnation*, 1896. Gifford, *The Incarnation*, 1897. Somerville, *St. Paul's Conception of Christ*, 1897. Hall, *Kenotic Theory*, 1898. Forsyth, *The Person and Place of Christ*, 1910. Weston, *The One Christ*, and art. ' Kenosis ' in Murray's *Illustr. BD.*

Among German commentaries on the Epistle the following will be found useful : De Wette, 1841, 3 ; B. Weiss, 1859 ; Von Soden, 1889 ; Lipsius, 1892 ; Klöpper, 1893 ; Haupt (in Meyer), 1902 ; Lueken (in J. Weiss), 1908 ; P. Ewald (in Zahn), 1908.

Frequent references are given in the notes to the very valuable *Vocabulary of the Greek Testament illustrated from Papyri and other Non-literary Sources*, by Moulton and Milligan, which has reached the word Θώραξ, and which Dr. Milligan is now carrying on since the lamented death of Dr. Moulton through enemy action in the war.

A COMMENTARY ON ST. PAUL'S EPISTLE TO THE PHILIPPIANS

i. 1, 2. THE SALUTATION

¹ Paul and Timotheus, the servants of Jesus Christ, to all the Saints in Christ Jesus which are at Philippi, with the Bishops and Deacons : ² Grace *be* unto you, and peace, from God our Father, and *from* the Lord Jesus Christ.

The Salutation in Philippians is somewhat longer than the one in 2 Thessalonians, and much longer than the one in I Thessalonians. Secular letters of the period have similar openings, but they are conventional, and have less fullness of wording, and still less fullness of meaning. What the Apostle meant by the Greek words which he uses, and what the better instructed among his converts would understand by them, is more than is conveyed to us by the English wording. For us they must be expanded.

¹ Paul and Timothy, well known to you as being, like yourselves, devoted bondservants of Christ Jesus, give greeting to the whole body of Christians in Philippi, whether Jews or Gentiles, who have been consecrated in Christ Jesus as a new Israel, together with their ministers—the bishops and deacons. ² We give you the Christian and the Jews greeting combined—grace, the source of all spiritual blessings, and peace, the end and issue of them all—desiring that you may receive them from God our Father and the Lord Jesus Christ.

1. As in the two Epistles to the Thessalonians and in the private letter to Philemon, St. Paul refrains from calling himself an Apostle, an official title which he uses at the opening of all his other letters, whether to Churches or to individual ministers, and on which he lays very great emphasis

1

in writing to the renegade Galatians.   The omission in these four cases indicates that the recipients of the letters had no need to be reminded of his Apostleship, and that he writes in a spirit of friendship, to exhort, instruct, and express affection and gratitude, rather than magisterially, to rebuke misconduct or correct misbelief.   All three of the letters to the Macedonian Christians, especially 1 Thessalonians and Philippians, are of this gentle and genial character.

In all three letters Timothy is joined with St. Paul in the Salutation, as being with him at the time of writing and as having been his colleague in the original mission to Macedonia.*   Timothy had visited Philippi at least once since then, and he is about to visit them again (ii. 19).   That Timothy was acting as the Apostle's amanuensis is possible, but not probable.   St. Paul would hardly have dictated ii. 19–23 to Timothy himself.   But, whereas in 1 and 2 Thessalonians the 1st pers. plur. is used almost uniformly throughout, and the ' we ' seems to embrace Timothy and Silvanus, here the 1st pers. sing. begins at once (' I thank,' not ' we thank ') and is continued throughout.   Timothy is dropped as completely as Sosthenes in 1 Corinthians ; and when he is mentioned again in ii. 19 it is as one who has no part in the contents of the letter.   See on 2 Thessalonians i. 1, p. 3.   *A vrai dire, Paul écrasa toujours ses disciples; ils ne jouèrent auprès de lui que le rôle de secrétaires, de serviteurs, de courriers.   Quand Paul était avec sa troupe, il existait seul.* Renan, *Saint Paul*, p. 565.

devoted bondservants of Christ Jesus] Cf. Rom. i. 1

---

* " The name is an Attic one and first occurs as the father of Conon the celebrated general (Thucyd. vii. 52) : the name afterwards often occurs in the literary and artistic history of Greece, and it is interesting to note its relation to Asia Minor.   It is not improbable that St. Timothy may have received his name out of compliment to the sculptor Timotheus, who was a contemporary of Praxiteles " (C. H. Hoole, *The Classical Element in the N.T.* p. 64).

The A.V. wavers between ' Timothy ' and ' Timotheus,' and the latter is often misread as three long syllables, instead of four syllables, one long and three short, thus Tĭmŏthĕŭs.   R.V. has ' Timothy ' throughout.

and Tit. i. 1. It is not servitude but *ownership* that is
indicated. Christians are free, but they are not their own,
they are not independent ; and in their dependence and
service they find their true freedom (Rom. vi. 22 ; 1 Cor.
vii. 22 ; 2 Cor. iii. 17). The expression δοῦλοι unites the
two missionaries, on the one hand with their Philippian
converts, on the other with the O.T. Prophets. Teachers
and taught were alike devoted to the service of God ; and
' servant of God ' or ' of the Lord ' is a frequent designation
of Prophets (Amos iii. 7 ; Jer. vii. 25, xxv. 4, xxix. 19 ;
Dan. ix. 6 ; Ezra ix. 11). The Greek word is commonly
δοῦλος, as here, but sometimes θεράπων, and sometimes
παῖς. It places the relation between God or Christ and
His ministers at a wider distance than θεράπων, and a still
wider than παῖς. On the other hand, it makes the tie
stronger. They are bound to Him for life ; they are His
property ; Gal. vi. 17. See Deissmann, *Light from the
Ancient East*, pp. 323 f. ; Thackeray, *Gram. of O.T. Grk.*
p. 8. The word here is perhaps meant to be in humble
contrast to ' the saints.'

of Christ Jesus] The words in this order are a proper
name indicating the glorified Christ, and the order is almost
peculiar to St. Paul. ' Jesus Christ ' may mean Jesus of
Nazareth who was the Messiah.

to the whole body of Christians] With remarkable persist-
ency St. Paul intimates that the Philippians are a united
whole, and that all of them have an equal share of his
affection and solicitude. He excludes no one from his love
and care, and there ought to be no dissensions among them ;
see *vv.* 3–8, 25–27, ii. 17, 26, iv. 21, 23. This feature in the
Epistle is unique.

who have been consecrated] This is the meaning of
' saints ' (ἅγιοι) ; not some who have attained to special
holiness of life, but all who have been admitted to the
Christian Church. As by circumcision the Jew was consecrated to Jehovah, so by baptism the Christian is consecrated
to Christ. In each case there is a covenant implying an
obligation to live a holy life. Cf. iv. 21, 22. Here again

O.T. phraseology is adopted, and adapted to N.T. use. The Israelites were set apart as a 'holy people'; Deut. vii. 6, xiv. 2, xxvi. 19, xxviii. 9; Isa. lxii. 12; Dan. xii. 7; cf. 1 Pet. ii. 9. The new Israel is set apart, in a simpler but higher way. This is emphasized by 'in Christ Jesus'; they are holy by spiritual union with Him; and this addition differentiates them from the Jewish ἅγιοι. On the uniformity of readings in the combination 'in Christ Jesus' and 'in Christ' see Sanday and Headlam on Rom. i. 1 and iii. 24.

The word ἅγιος is rare in classical Greek.

with the bishops and deacons] Neither word has the article, σὺν ἐπισκόποις καὶ διακόνοις, which *perhaps* indicates that St. Paul did not know them personally. But he knew that there were such ministers, and he wishes his readers to understand that he addresses every one, officials included. We have σύν, which implies a closer connexion than μετά : Simcox, *Lan. of the N.T.* p. 150; *una cum* (Beza). The reading συνεπισκόποις, though accepted by Chrysostom, Theodore of Mopsuestia, Theophylact, and Cassiodorus, is " meaningless and indefensible " (Ellicott). Translators differ considerably; Vincent, 'with the superintendents and ministers'; Way, 'along with their Church-overseers and church stewards'; Weymouth, 'with the ministers of the Church and their assistants'; 20th Cent. N.T., 'with the Presidents and Assistant-Officers'; Cunnington, 'with overseers and deacons.' Colloquially we might say, 'bishops, deacons, and all.'

This is the earliest use of these terms as the names of two distinct classes of Church officials. Among their functions they probably managed the funds of the congregation, and had been instrumental in sending financial help to the Apostle. This may be the reason why he mentions them here, as an indirect acknowledgment of their trouble on his behalf. The Philippians would know why they are mentioned. On the one hand, there is an advance on 1 Thess. v. 12, where the single article shows that only one class of officials is indicated (see note there). On the other, the plural shows that the condition of a monarchical bishop, distinct from and above the presbyters, has not yet been reached. In the N.T., as in Clement of Rome (xlii. 4, xliv. 1), ἐπίσκοπος and πρεσβύτερος are convertible terms. *Hic 'episcopos' presbyteros intellegimus; non enim in una urbe plures episcopi esse potuissent* (Pelagius). Theodore says the same, and remarks that presbyters would not have been omitted if bishops had meant the superior order.* That the Seven in Acts vi. were the original deacons is doubtful; Acts xxi. 8 Philip, one of the Seven, is not called 'the deacon,' but 'the evangelist.' See Lightfoot, *Philippians*, pp. 95 f. ; Moulton and Milligan, *Vocabulary of the Grk. Test.* p. 149 ; Hastings' *DAC.* artt. 'Bishops' and 'Church Government.'

The ' bishops and deacons ' are mentioned after the whole body of Christians, just as in Acts xv. 4 ' the apostles and elders ' are mentioned after 'the Church.' Contrast Heb. xiii. 24. The order is indifferent ; and the curious explanation of Aquinas, that "shepherds go behind their flocks," is not required.

2. grace and peace] This combination of Western and Eastern salutations is found in all the Pauline Epistles, with 'mercy' inserted between the two in the Pastorals. It occurs in 1 and 2 Peter, 2 John, and Revelation, and we do not know who originated it. It evidently became widely current at an early date. See Charles on Rev. i. 4. In the O.T., 'grace' (χάρις) is frequent in the Wisdom Books ; and in the N.T. is extraordinarily frequent in the Pauline, especially of God's favour to man as manifested in His incarnate Son, a favour which generates peace of mind. ' Peace ' is not the mere absence of anxiety, or the mere cessation of antagonism between man and man. It is the cessation of antagonism between man and God, the product of permanent reconciliation. See on 2 Thess. i. 2 ; J. A. Robinson, *Ephesians*, p. 221 ; Sanday and

* In the Ep. of Polycarp to the Philippians there are ' presbyters ' and ' deacons,' but no ' bishops.'

Headlam on Rom. i. 5 ; Renan, *Hibbert Lectures*, 1880, p. 11 ; T. R. Glover, *The Jesus of History*, p. 206.

God our Father and the Lord Jesus Christ] This equal emphasis on the Father and Christ is very remarkable and very frequent in the Pauline Epistles from first to last, and is not confined to them. It is specially remarkable for the transfer of the Greek equivalent of the ineffable ' Jehovah ' to Jesus Christ as His usual title. St. Paul rarely uses it of the Father, but constantly of the Messiah. In these four chapters it is thus used 14 times. See Renan, *Saint Paul*, p. 274 ; Briggs, *The Messiah of the Apostles*, p. 86 ; Hort on 1 Pet. i. 3 ; Simcox, *Lang. of N.T.* p. 49 ; Case, *Evolution of Early Christianity*, pp. 112, 236, 356.

i. 3–26. HISTORICAL AND PERSONAL

The first main portion of the letter begins here, and it has two sections, one concerning the Philippians, and one concerning himself. These two subjects alternate in this intimate and affectionate letter, and at last are blended together. We have here i. 3–11 Thanksgiving and Prayer for the Philippians, and 12–26 the Apostle's Circumstances and Feelings.

i. 3–11. THANKSGIVING AND PRAYER FOR THE PHILIPPIANS.

[3] I thank my God upon every remembrance of you, [4] Always in every prayer of mine for you all making request with joy, [5] For your fellowship in the Gospel from the first day until now ; [6] Being confident of this very thing, that he which hath begun a good work in you, will perform it until the day of Jesus Christ : [7] Even as it is meet for me to think this of you all, because I have you in my heart, inasmuch as both in my bonds, and in the defence and confirmation of the Gospel, ye are all partakers of my grace. [8] For God is my record, how greatly I long after you all, in the bowels of Jesus Christ. [9] And this I pray, that your love may abound yet more and more in knowledge, and in all judgment. [10] That

(A.V.). For ' begin . . . complete ' cf. 2 Cor. viii. 6 ; Gal.
iii. 3.

till the Day of Christ's Return] ' Right up to the Day ';
also called the ' Day of the Lord ' (see on 1 Thess. v. 2) and
' that Day ' (see on 2 Thess. i. 10), a dominant thought with
the first Christians. The expression suggests a day of trial
in which every one's work will be tested (1 Cor. iii. 13), and
this needs to be stated in English. St. Paul nowhere says
that he will live till then ; he merely suggests that he may be
among those who will do so. As to the details of the ' Day
of Jesus Christ'—an expression peculiar to this Epistle—
he has no fixed eschatological system ; but he believed that
the Day was near. Here, as often, we have a difference of
reading between ' Christ Jesus ' and ' Jesus Christ '; but
not when ' in ' precedes.

7. I have full justification] Lit. ' Even as it is just for
me,' καθώς ἐστιν δίκαιον ἐμοί. The pronoun is emphatic.

for being thus minded] Or ' to feel this,' τοῦτο φρονεῖν, a
Pauline verb, very frequent in this letter and in Romans.
See on ii. 2. He is sure that his converts will have neither
so much trust in themselves as to suppose that it was in
their own strength that they began the Christian life, nor
so much distrust in God as to fear that after all He will fail
them. Cf. ii. 12, 13.

in my heart] There is no possessive pronoun in the Greek
(ἐν τῇ καρδίᾳ), and the two personal pronouns might be
transposed. Either ' I have you in my heart ' or ' you have
me in your heart ' is possible grammatically. The context
(v. 8) and the order of the words decide for the former.

had fellowship with me] ' Shared it with me.' ' Sympa-
thized with me ' is inadequate ; actual fellow-suffering is
meant. See on iv. 14. Compounds with σύν are frequent
in Paul; in this letter we have συνκοινωνός, συνέχομαι,
συνψύχος, συνχαίρω, συνεργός, συνστρατιώτης, συμμορφιζόμενος, σύμμορφος, συνμιμήτης, συνλαμβάνω, συνκοινωνέω.

in the sufferings of my imprisonment] Two things are
coupled (ἔν τε . . . καὶ ἐν), and two aspects are given of
the second. The first sums up the Apostle's suffering ;

the second describes his work under two aspects—his
defence of the Gospel against criticism and his confirmation
of it by argument.   But the two aspects are treated as one,
under one and the same article (ἐν τῇ ἀπολογίᾳ καὶ βεβαιώσει),
they sum up missionary effort.   The 'defence' might
refer to pleading before the Imperial Court at Rome, as
Zahn contends; but this is less likely; cf. v. 16.   For
βεβαίωσις see M. and M., *Vocabulary*, p. 108; Deissmann,
Bible Studies, p. 104; and cf. Heb. vi. 16.

of the grace] 'Grace' has the article (τῆς χάριτος) and
means the grace of God, a Divine privilege; 2 Cor. iv. 15;
Gal. v. 4; Eph. ii. 8, iv. 7.   This 'grace' is the ground of
the 'justification' mentioned above.   Vulg. has *gaudii*;
confusion of χάριτος with χαρᾶς.   The Divine privilege
in this case is their fellowship in his sufferings and in the
sufferings of Christ; cf. ἐχαρίσθη in v. 29.*

8. for I call God to witness] Not 'ıecord' (A.V.).   The
'for' (γάρ) refers to the truth of the declaration of his
affectionate remembrance of his converts.   He often uses
this solemn asseveration with regard to what was hidden
from human eyes, sometimes to repel charges or suspicions,
as in 2 Cor. i. 23 and Gal. i. 20, sometimes, as here and Rom.
i. 9, to emphasize his intense affection.   Cf. Rom. ix. 1;
2 Cor. xi. 31.   "In regard to what was hidden, to whom
could he appeal but to God?" (Aug. *Ep.* cxxvi. 10).   No
other reason need be sought.

yearn after you all] The compound ἐπιποθῶ is probably
to some extent intensive, although the ἐπί marks the direction of the longing rather than its intensity; cf. ii. 26,
and see on 1 Thess. iii. 6.   The yearning may include
their eternal salvation; it is no mere human affection.
Il s'était mis en état de ne se réjouir du bien qu'on lui

* *La seule chose qui depende de nous, c'est de rendre nos souffrances
meritoires : mais souffrir, ou ne pas souffrir, n'est point laissé à notre
choix.   Nous sommes ingénieux à nous priver nous-mêmes de tout
le mérite de nos souffrances.   Ce que damne la plupart des hommes
ne sont pas les plaisirs seulement ; c'est encore l'usage peu chrétien
qu'ils font de leurs peines* (Massillon, Sermon for the 2nd S. in Advent).

faisait, que pour l'amour de ceux qui le faisaient (Bossuet).

with the tenderness of Christ Jesus] ' With a heart which is one with the heart of Messiah Christ ' (Way). ' With tender Christian affection ' (Weymouth). It is a spiritual yearning. ' In the bowels ' is a clumsy mistranslation of σπλάγχνα, frequent in A.V. The σπλ. included the heart, lungs, and liver, as distinct from the intestines or bowels. The Greek poets regarded the σπλ. as the seat of the stormy affections, as anger and love ; the Hebrews as the seat of the tender affections, as pity and charity. Here the meaning is much the same as ' heart ' in *v.* 7 ; but we have two words in Greek and need two words in English. ' Breast ' would serve here, but not in ii. 1 ; ' tenderness ' will do in both places. No one word will suit all the passages. Here and ii. 1 R.V. has ' tender mercies ' ; Col. iii. 12 and Philem. 12, 20 ' heart ' ; 2 Cor. vi. 12 ' affections ' ; vii. 15 ' inward affection ' ; 1 Jn. iii. 17 ' compassion.' On St. Paul's " mystic genitive," expressing mystic fellowship, see on 2 Thess. ii. 18, iii. 5 ; Deissmann, *St. Paul*, p. 140. Wiclif thinks that *viscera Christi* are the ordinances contained in the Church, which ought to be revived, *Sermo* lvi. Better Bengel ; *In Paulo non Paulus vivit sed Christus ; quare Paulus in Christi movetur visceribus.* See Rostron, *Christology*, p. 138 ; Suicer, II. 997.

We say ' *in* the heart,' ' *with* the tenderness ' ; in the Greek we have ἐν in both verses. In late Greek ἐν is a hard-worked preposition.

We may note again how repeatedly in this section St. Paul insists that what he says applies to *all* his converts. There are no exceptions. There had been disputes of some kind (iv. 2, 3), which he deplored, and about which he would not take sides. In his estimation and affection they all stand high. The affectionate words lead on naturally to prayer for them.

The prayer portion illuminates the meaning of ' Pray without ceasing,' 1 Thess. v. 17. All work must be done, all life must be lived, with a *sense of the presence of God* which is the spirit of prayer. The Apostle is ever conscious

that his work cannot prosper without the blessing of God,
for which from time to time he definitely prays. "Nowhere does this brave, strenuous, kind and loving person-
ality stand forth revealed more clearly than in his prayers"
(Weinel, *St. Paul, the Man and his Work*, p. 129).

9. **this is the substance**] What follows looks back to the
statement that he constantly prays for the Philippians
(*v.* 4). *Gaudium ad praeteritum tempus refertur, precatio ad
futurum. Redit ad precationem, quam obiter tantum uno verbo
attigerat* (Calvin).

that] The ἵνα gives the purport rather than the purpose of the prayer, as in 1 Thess. iii. 1 ; Col. i. 9.

your love] Possibly love for one another is specially meant,
but ἡ ἀγάπη seems to be used here, as in 1 Cor. xiii., for
'love' in its fullest sense. It comes first, before 'knowledge'
and 'discernment.' Prayer for its increase implies that it
already exists. For ἔτι cf. Heb. vii. 15.

more and more] For the characteristic addition cf. *v.* 23 ; 1
Thess. iv. 1, 10 ; 2 Cor. vii. 13. Here we have ἔτι μᾶλλον
καὶ μᾶλλον, which in conjunction with the special verb in
the present tense (περισσεύῃ) conveys the idea of extreme
and continually increasing abundance. He can hardly
find words strong enough to express the affectionate large-
ness of his requests for them. *Ignis in apostolo nunquam
dicit, Sufficit* (Bengel).

in perfect knowledge] It is another characteristic of St.
Paul that he always desires that his converts should have,
by instruction and experience, full appreciation of the real
meaning of Christian belief and duty. Such is specially
the case in the four Epistles of this group. Without these,
love may go grievously astray. Misty thought, emotional
conduct, and indiscriminate good nature are perilous.
As in Eph. i. 17, iv. 13 ; Col. i. 9, 10, ii. 2, iii. 10 ; Philem.
6, we have the compound ἐπίγνωσις, which perhaps generally
implies advanced and full knowledge. Here the ἐπι- corre-
sponds to the πάσῃ before αἰσθήσει. See Evans on 1 Cor.
xiii. 12, Lightfoot on Col. i. 9, and Maurice Jones here.

unfailing discernment] Every kind of sensitiveness with

regard to Christian feeling and conduct. The converts should become experts in spiritual things, and know instinctively what matters, and what does not matter, in thought and action. A new sense, a moral taste, is acquired ; Heb. v. 14. As regards such things, the whole Church must (as Newman has said), " like its Divine Founder during the time of *His* education, be ever in the midst of the doctors, both hearing them and asking them questions." Αἴσθησις occurs nowhere else in N.T. Cf. Prov. i. 4, 22, ii. 10. A.V. has 'judgment' or 'sense.' See M. and M., *Vocabulary*, p. 14.

It is love that is to have this knowledge and discernment. Christian love is not blind, and while it increases, it is regulated. The Philippians' affection for the Apostle ought not to make them gloomy about his condition.

10. **so that you can**] For εἰς τό of the result cf. 1 Thess. ii. 12, iii. 10 ; 2 Thess. i. 5 ; 2 Cor. viii. 6. Burton, *N.T. Moods and Tenses*, § 409.

with sureness approve] Because δοκιμάζειν means approval after a testing investigation ; 1 Thess. ii. 3, v. 21. It is assumed that approval leads to action. M. and M., *Vocabulary*, p. 167.

the things which are really excellent] The same phrase, δοκιμάζειν τὰ διαφέροντα, occurs Rom. ii. 15, and in both places opinions differ as to the meaning ; see R.V. and margin. For τὰ διαφέροντα may mean either ' things that surpass, that are excellent,' or ' things that differ.' If the latter is adopted, δοκιμάζειν refers to the testing rather than to the approval which is the result of the testing. But it does not require much spiritual knowledge and discernment to test things which differ. Such powers are much more necessary to decide with sureness what things are really excellent and worthy of adoption in practice ; τίνα μὲν καλά, τίνα δὲ κρείττονα (Theodoret) ; *probare potiora* (Vulg.). 1 Cor. abounds with instances of the Apostle's moral taste and tact.

and thus be] The second ἵνα depends on the preceding clause, and not on the first clause in *v.* 9. A repetition of ' I pray ' (προσεύχομαι) is not to be understood.

free from stain and from stumbling] The derivation of εἰλικρινεῖς remains an unsolved problem ; but it certainly means ' unsullied,' "pure ' ; cf. 2 Pet. iii. 10 and see on 2 Cor. i. 12. Trench, *Syn.* § lxxxv. It is probable that ἀπρόσκοπος is here intransitive as in a speech of St. Paul in Acts xxiv. 16. So also in papyri, ' free from hurt or harm.' See also Suicer. But ' without *giving* offence,' ' without *causing* to stumble,' as in 1 Cor. x. 32 and Ecclus. xxxii. 21, makes good sense ; ' spotless ' in the sight of God, and ' harmless ' in the sight of men. M. and M., *Vocabulary*, pp. 72, 183 f.

fit for the Day of Christ] Or ' with a view to,' ' against,' εἰς ἡμέραν. The Day of Judgment is meant, as in *v.* 6 and ii. 16. It is their condition in reference to God that is in the Apostle's mind ; on that Day there must be nothing to offend Him. His prayer, like his thanksgiving (*v.* 6), looks forward to that decisive moment, which would be often in his mind as years, and especially years of imprisonment, passed. Case, *The Evolution of Early Christianity*, p. 111.

11. as being filled] Perf. part. (πεπληρωμένοι) ; they have been filled and the fullness abides.

fruit of righteousness] The fruit which righteousness produces ; Amos vi. 12 ; Prov. xi. 30 ; Jas. iii. 18. ' Righteousness ' means fulfilment of duties to God and to man.

not by our power] This is the point of stating that the fruit of righteousness is won ' through Jesus Christ.' The Philippians must not suppose that they can attain this rich fruit by their own unaided effort and merit. Only through union with Christ can this be done ; iv. 13 ; 2 Cor. xii. 9. ' The branch cannot bear fruit of itself.' *

to promote the glory of God] Bearing much fruit is specially to His glory ; Jn. xv. 8. This is the true end of all Christian action ; 1 Cor. x. 31 ; 1 Pet. iv. 11. No other end, however holy, can supersede it. Cf. ' That they might be called trees of righteousness, the planting of the Lord, that He might

---

* A heathen does good work, yet not consciously through Christ ; a hypocrite does good work, yet not for God's praise, but man's.

be glorified,' Is. lxi. 3. For δόξα see Kennedy, *St. Paul's Conception of the Last Things*, p. 299 ; Milligan, *Thessalonians*, p. 27.

our praise] ' Glory ' and ' praise ' are not mere synonyms. ' Glory ' refers to Divine grace exhibited in holy lives, ' praise ' to human gratitude for this gift ; Eph. i. 6, 12. See Hort on the combination of the two words in 1 Pet. i. 7, and M. and M., *Vocabulary*, p. 227.

Having thanked God for his readers' happy condition and prayed for their further progress, he now tells them about himself.

i. 12–26. HISTORICAL AND PERSONAL

We have here a brief description of St. Paul's bodily and mental condition during his imprisonment in Rome, and of the somewhat chequered furtherance of the Gospel there. The Philippians must not suppose that his imprisonment has put a stop to this furtherance : on the contrary, it has helped it, especially among the troops of the Imperial Guard. Some preachers are unfriendly ; but even this will prove a blessing through the Philippians' prayers, which he is sure to have. His sufferings inspire friendly preachers with fresh zeal. He expects to be set free and to visit the Philippians again.

It is possible that the Philippians had sent a letter of inquiry and sympathy, in which they spoke of their pride in him (i. 26) and apologized for their slowness in sending help (iv. 10). More probably Epaphroditus brought messages from them.

The paragraph consists of three sections, each of which forms a complete sentence in the Greek ; 12–14, 15–20, 21–26. It is convenient to break two of these into shorter sentences in English.

i. 12–14. RESULTS OF THE APOSTLE'S CAPTIVITY.

12 But I would ye should understand, brethren, that the things which happened unto me have fallen out rather unto the furtherance

of the Gospel. ¹³ So that my bonds in Christ are manifest in all
the palace, and in all other *places*. ¹⁴ And many of the brethren
in the Lord, waxing confident in my bonds, are much more bold
to speak the word without fear.

This section can, without serious disadvantage, be kept
as one sentence in paraphrasing.

¹² Now I am afraid that you may be under some apprehension about
myself and my doings, and I therefore would have you understand,
Brethren, that my condition of captivity, so far from being an impedi-
ment to the spread of the Gospel, has really come to be a help to its
advance ; ¹³ so that the fact of my being in bonds became, in the
power of Christ, a manifest influence among all the soldiers of the
Imperial Guards and all the rest ; ¹⁴ and also so that the large majority
of the brethren here, having found in the Lord a ground for confidence
in my endurance of my bonds, have gained still more abundant courage
to speak the word of God and to speak it fearlessly.

12. **I therefore would have you understand**] St. Paul
was very sensitive as to what his converts might think of
him, his circumstances, and his work. This feeling is
apparent in 1 Thess. ii. 1–12 and 2 Thess. ii. 2, iii. 7–9.
It is still more apparent in 2 Cor. i. 12, iii. 1, iv. 7, vi. 10,
x. 1–xii. 18. When the Apostle was for years in prison,
his converts would be specially perplexed ; ' An ambassador
in chains ' (Eph. vi. 20) was such a contradiction. Therefore in the Epistles of the Captivity this feature is conspicuous ; Eph. iii. 1–13 ; Col. i. 24–29 ; Philem. 9, 13. But we
cannot safely infer from what is said here that the easy
method of imprisonment of Acts xxviii. 30 had ended and a
more severe kind been imposed. With ' would have you
understand ' cf. ' do not wish you to remain in ignorance,'
1 Thess. iv. 13 ; 1 Cor. x. 1 ; 2 Cor. i. 8. In these phrases
θέλω is more common than βούλομαι, which we have here,
and this exact phrase occurs nowhere else. Βούλομαι
implies " will with premeditation " ; Hort on Jas. iv. 4 ; and
here ' to understand ' is emphatic. Such expressions are
so common in correspondence that we are not surprised
to find them in secular letters preserved in papyri. See
M. and M., *Vocabulary*, p. 115. We say in commercial
prose ' I beg· to inform you.'

Brethren] The address occurs six times in this affectionate letter. For ἀδελφοί as members of a religious guild see M. and M., p. 9 ; Harnack, *Mission and Expansion of Christianity*, I. pp. 405 ff. ; see also Kennedy, *Sources of N.T. Grk.* p. 95.

my condition] He does not say ' my sufferings and perils,' but ' my circumstances' (τὰ κατ' ἐμέ), as in Eph. vi. 21 ; Col. iv. 7 ; cf. Tobit x. 8. A. T. Robertson, *Grammar of Greek N.T.* p. 608.

so far from being] ' As you may be supposing.' Perhaps his enemies said that his prolonged imprisonment was proof of God's displeasure. This use of μᾶλλον, ' rather than the contrary,' is idiomatic. Vulg. has *magis*, but *potius* would be better. Winer, p. 304.

has come to be] Cf. Wisd. xv. 5 εἰς ὄνειδος ἔρχεται. Vulg. has *venerunt* ; better *evenerunt*.

advance] Προκοπή (1 Tim. iv. 15 ; Ecclus. li. 17 ; 2 Macc. viii. 8) is a military metaphor from removing trees and other obstacles (προκόπτειν) before an advancing army.

13. **became in the power of Christ**] A.V. wrongly connects this phrase with ' bonds,' and in ' are manifest ' ignores the change from perfect to aorist.* On the thoroughly Pauline expression ἐν Χριστῷ, which sums up the relation of the believer to the Saviour, see Sanday and Headlam on Rom. vi. 11 ; Headlam, *St. Paul and Christianity*, pp. 143 f. ; Pfleiderer, *Paulinism*, I. pp. 197 ff.

among all the soldiers of the imperial guards] Lit. ' in the whole of the *praetorium*.' Does this mean a particular residence, and if so, which ? Or, a particular body of men ? *Praetorium* meant originally ' the praetor's or general's tent in a camp,' *i.e.* ' head-quarters.' When the praetors became civil magistrates in Rome and were often sent to provinces as governors, their official residence in the province was called *praetorium* (Matt. xxvii. 27 ; Mk. xv. 16 ; Jn. xviii. 28, 33 ; Acts xxiii. 35). That is not the meaning here ; the

---

* That ἐν Χριστῷ must go with φανεροί, and that ' all the rest ' means all who visited St. Paul in his dwelling, is pointed out by Wieseler, *Chronologie*, p. 457.

praetorium which St. Paul influenced was in Rome. On
the assumption that it means a *place*, two hypotheses are
advocated. (1) The Imperial residence on the Palatine,
' the palace ' (A.V.). The opinion of Greek Fathers (who
are not good authorities about Roman technical terms)
cannot make this explanation probable. Nowhere is the
word used in this sense ; nor is it likely that it ever was so
used, or that St. Paul, who was in Rome at the time of writing, has here made an ignorant blunder. (2) The camp
established for the praetorian cohorts by Tiberius, traces
of which survive near the present Porta Pia. This meaning
also lacks authority. On the assumption that it means
persons rather than a place, two other hypotheses are advocated. (3) The Praetorian regiments or Imperial Guards.
There is abundant evidence (Livy, Tacitus, Suetonius,
Pliny, Josephus and inscriptions) that the word was used
in this sense. Evidently ' and all the rest ' points to *persons*
rather than a place. Lightfoot and most moderns adopt
this view. (4) Ramsay, *St. Paul the Traveller*, p. 357,
follows Mommsen in thinking that the *persons connected
with the imperial court* which tried St. Paul are meant.
The Apostle might have impressed them. Seeing, however,
that he was imprisoned in Rome for two years, that a soldier
was always with him, and that the soldier was frequently
changed, his opportunities of influencing large numbers of
the soldiers must have been far greater. He was in the
custody of the Prefect of the Praetorians, and in the course
of two years the same soldiers must often have sat with
him for hours. *Sa cellule de prisonnier devint un foyer
de prédication ardente. . . . La prison de Paul fut ainsi
plus féconde, que ne l'avait été sa libre activité. Ses chaines
était à elles comme une prédication* (Renan, *L'Antechrist*,
pp. 9, 10). See Lightfoot's detached note and Hastings'
DAC. artt. ' Guard ' and ' Palace.' All these interpreta-
tions point to Rome, not Caesarea, as the place where the
letter was written. Cf. iv. 22.

all the rest] An indefinite expression (καὶ τοῖς λοιποῖς
πᾶσιν), meaning that there were many other persons in

Rome who were influenced by the 'ambassador in chains.'
It was evident to all who visited this interesting prisoner
that he was no vulgar criminal or dangerous leader of
revolt. Cf. 2 Cor. xiii. 8 ; Col. i. 23. There is no need
to confine it to the rest of the *soldiers*. We all use similar
hyperbole, knowing that it will not be understood literally.
" The words intimate a wide personal influence " (Moule).
' The *palace* and all other *places* ' (A.V.) cannot stand.

14. **the large majority**] Cf. 1 Cor. ix. 19 ; 2 Cor. ii. 6,
iv. 15. This is another good result of the imprisonment.
'Many' (A.V.) may *perhaps* stand for τοὺς πλείονας in
spite of the article ; Blass, § 44, 3.

having found in the Lord] A.V. and R.V. connect ' in the
Lord' with ' brethren,' which has little point. ' Brethren '=
' Christians,' who of course are ' in the Lord.' In Col.
iv. 7 the brother is ' *beloved* in the Lord ' ; in Col. i. 2 the
brethren are ' *faithful* in Christ.' Here it is the *confidence*
that is ' rooted in the Lord.' Nowhere is ' in the Lord '
connected with ' brethren.' Cf. ii. 24 ; 2 Thess. iii. 4 ;
Gal. v. 10. Respecting ' confidence ' (πεποιθότας) see on
i. 6. For the construction cf. 2 Cor. x. 7.

my bonds] His endurance of them was evidence that the
Gospel was something worth suffering for. ' The word
of God is not bound,' 2 Tim. ii. 9.

more abundant courage] Through contemplating the
heroic endurance of the prisoner.* Courage had already
been exhibited by them, and in him they had a pledge of
their own victory, *signus victoriae nostrae habentes* (Calvin).
All Christians are regarded as ' speaking the word of God.'

the word of God] Following inferior MSS. the A.V. omits
' of God.' Cf. Acts iv. 31 ; 1 Cor. xiv. 36 ; 2 Cor. iv. 2 ;
Col. i. 25.

fearlessly] The Apostle harps on courage and confidence.

---

* Moreover, " the clearer it became that nothing of a suspicious
character could be alleged against his work, the bolder they could
become in preaching, without fear that they would be suspected
of any crime " (B. Weiss *ad loc.*).   Cf. ἀκωλύτως, Acts xxviii. 31.

i. 15–20.   THE FRIENDLY AND THE UNFRIENDLY PREACHERS.

[15] Some indeed preach Christ even of envy and strife, and some also of good will.   [16] The one preach Christ of contention, not sincerely, supposing to add affliction to my bonds :   [17] But the other of love, knowing that I am set for the defence of the Gospel.   [18] What then ? Notwithstanding, every way, whether in pretence, or in truth, Christ is preached, and I therein do rejoice, yea, and will rejoice. [19] For I know that this shall turn to my salvation through your prayer, and the supply of the spirit of Jesus Christ, [20] According to my earnest expectation and my hope, that in nothing I shall be ashamed, but that with all boldness, as always, *so* now also Christ shall be magnified in my body, whether it be by life or by death.

We have here a second paradox.   It was paradoxical that the imprisonment of the Apostle should tend to the spread of the Gospel.   It was a still greater paradox that the Gospel of love and peace should be preached out of envy and strife.

[15] I say that the majority of the brethren are inspired by my sufferings to speak the word of God nobly.   The truth is that some whom I could mention are actually preaching the Christ of envy and strife, while others do so also of benevolent purpose both to the cause and me.   [16] The latter do this out of love to me, because they know that I am set here by God to defend the Gospel, [17] while the former proclaim [the] Christ out of partisanship, with sadly mixed motives, thinking in this way to increase the pressure of my bonds.   [18] Then what is the result ?   Only that in every kind of way, whether by a mere show of disinterestedness, or with what is truly such, Christ is being proclaimed ; and therein I rejoice.   Yes, and I shall go on rejoicing. [19] Surely that is the right thing to do ; for I know that all this chequered success and suffering, so far from injuring me, will conduce to my salvation here and hereafter, through your entreaty for me, and the consequent bountiful supply of the Spirit of Jesus Christ. [20] All this is in accordance with my intense anticipation and hope that no atom of shame will be found in me ; on the contrary, that with every form of boldness of speech, as on all previous occasions, so also in the present crisis, Christ will be magnified in my person, whether I continue to live or am sentenced to death.

15. **some whom I could mention**] This use of τινες occurs in all four groups of the Pauline Epistles ; 2 Thess. iii. 11 ;

1 Cor. iv. 18, xv. 12 ; 2 Cor. iii. 1, x. 2 ; Gal. i. 7 ; Tim.
i. 3, 19, etc., A. T. Robertson, *Gr.* pp. 743, 1200.

actually] A frequent use of καί : Gal. ii. 13, 17.

of envy and strife] Through (διά) envious and contentious
dispositions. Cf. Mk. xv. 10 ; Mt. xxii. 18. Envy and
strife are often in combination ; Rom. i. 29 ; Gal. v. 20 ;
1 Tim. vi. 4. This strange contradiction is not rare. Religious teaching often aims more at the discomfiture of those
who dissent from us than at bringing men to Christ. Calvin
says that in this he had the same experience as St. Paul.
' *The* Christ ' may indicate that these missionaries were
Judaizers, who chiefly insisted on the fact that Jesus was
the promised Messiah.

benevolent purpose] The meaning of the Biblical word
εὐδοκία varies according to the context. Here the opposi-
tion to ' envy and strife ' requires ' kindly intention ' or
' goodwill ' ; Eph. i. 5, 9 ; Ecclus. i. 27, ii. 16, xii. 17, etc.
The ' goodwill ' is general ; not merely to the Apostle,
but also to his work. Cf. ii. 13. *Propensa voluntate* (Beza).

16. **The latter**] Inverted order ; chiasmus is frequent
in the Pauline Epistles. See on 2 Cor. ii. 16, vi. 8, ix. 6,
xiii. 3 ; etc. A.V. transposes *vv.* 16 and 17.

I am set here] Or, ' I am appointed ' (κεῖμαι) ; ' this is
why God keeps me in Rome.' Cf. 1 Thess. iii. 3 ; Lk. ii.
34 ; Ecclus. xxxix. 29. ' Lying inactive ' is not the meaning ; rather ' posted as a sentinel.'

to defend] Not ' to give an *account* ' of his ministry to God,
as Chrysostom and others understand εἰς ἀπολογίαν. See
on *v.* 7.

17. **proclaim**] A.V. has ' preach ' for both κηρύσσειν and
καταγγέλλειν.

Christ out of partisanship] The words are in proximity for
the sake of contrast ; what has partisanship or intrigue
to do with Christ ? The words ' proclaim Christ ' are
rather superfluous, and may be inserted for the sake of
the contrast. Ἐριθεία is not connected with ἔρις, but
with ἔριθος, ' a hired labourer.' Hence ' electioneering
with hired canvassers,' and so ' party spirit.' A.V. has

'strife,' as if from ἔρις.   See on 2 Cor. xii. 20, and Lightfoot
on Gal. v. 20.*

with sadly mixed motives] Lit. 'not purely,' οὐχ ἁγνῶς.
Some of their motives were utterly base ; καλὰ μέν, οὐ
καλῶς δέ. Theodoret ;   *rem castam non caste*, Augustine.
P. Ewald's proposal to make οὐχ ἁγνῶς apply to *both* the
parties is surprising.

think] There is marked contrast between εἰδότες
and οἰόμενοι ; the friendly preachers *know*, the unfriendly
ones *suppose*.   Οἰόμενοι suggests that the thinking is
erroneous ; Jas. i. 7 ; 1 Macc. v. 61 ; 2 Macc. v. 21.   Chrysostom and Theodoret surmise that these unfriendly
preachers said that Paul's vigorous preaching would excite
Nero to persecute.   Similarly Pelagius and Erasmus.

in this way] Present infinitive, not future.

to increase the pressure] Θλίψις, commonly rendered
'affliction' or 'tribulation,' Vulg. *pressura* or *tribulatio*,
implies pressure, and in classical Greek is used of actual
crushing.   Here the idea of pressure is appropriate.   These
unfriendly preachers suppose that they aggravate the galling
of the chains.   *Vincula jam pressura erat ; afflicto afflictionem
addere putabant* (Bengel).   But the true reading is ἐγείρειν,
'to raise,' not ἐπιφέρειν, 'to add' (A.V.).

18. **Then what is the result?**] Lit. 'For what? ' or 'What
then ? '   'Well, what of that ? '   This usage of τί γάρ
is classical.   Cf. Rom. iii. 3.   Vaughan follows Meyer and
transfers the interrogation to the end of the sentence ; 'For
what is it but that every way, etc.'   That is, 'The result
is nothing but this.'

---

* Kennedy thinks that '*selfish*' ambition may be the prevailing
meaning in N.T.   Possibly they gloated over the fact that they
were free to preach where and when they pleased, while his opportunities were greatly curtailed.   Envious themselves, they thought
that this would make him envious.   That they hoped " to increase
the severity of his imprisonment *by exciting the jealousy of the
Court* " cannot be the meaning.   He was not the founder of
the Church in Rome, and they may have regarded him as an
intruder.

only that] They meant to produce affliction, and they have caused joy. Cf. Acts xx. 23. Some texts here omit πλήν and some (with more probability) omit ὅτι.

in every kind of way] Cf. 2 Thess. iii. 16 ; Rom. iii. 2.

a mere show] Or, ' ostensible motive ' (προφάσει). As in 1 Thess. ii. 5, this would be disinterestedness. The word commonly implies that the ostensible motive is insincere ; Acts xxvii. 30. Vulg. has *per occasionem*, which is not the meaning ; Beza *in speciem*.

therein I rejoice] The punctuation is uncertain. Apparently St. Paul checks himself here ; it seems so strange to rejoice at insincere preaching of Christ. But on the whole he feels justified and decides that he may go on rejoicing. This requires a full stop after ' rejoice ' and after ' rejoicing.' But it is possible to place only a comma after ' rejoicing ' and connect closely with what follows ; ' I shall go on rejoicing, for I know that, etc.' Both ways make good sense. The punctuation of A.V. and R.V. is less forcible. See on 2 Cor. xi. 1, where there is similar doubt about ἀλλὰ καί and punctuation.

These outbursts of joy from one who for years had been a prisoner are remarkable. But Renan says with truth, *En somme peu d'années dans la vie de l'apôtre furent plus heureuses que celles-ci* (*L'Antechrist*, p. 17). Moreover, this spirit of resignation, which is not found in Galatians or 2 Corinthians, is natural enough towards the end of a very chequered imprisonment. See Augustine, Letter to Vincentius, *Ep*. XCIII. iv. 15. We learn from Chrysostom, Theodore, and Theodoret that this passage was misinterpreted to mean that St. Paul did not approve of attacks upon heresy. But in this case it was not the teaching, but the spirit of the teachers, that was wrong.

19. **All this**] This perplexing combination of what is wholly satisfactory with what is mainly very much the reverse.

will conduce to] ' Will turn out to ' ; *non modo non in pressuram* (Bengel) : Lk. xx. 13 ; 2 Macc. ix. 24. Here we have a quotation from Job xiii. 16 ; cf. xv. 3. Quotations

D

from Job are rare in N.T. Cf. 1 Thess. v. 22 ; Rom. xi.
35 ; Lk. i. 52.

my salvation] In its widest sense, as is shown by what
follows respecting the Holy Spirit. Chrysostom limits
it to deliverance from peril ; but cf. *v.* 28, ii. 22, and the
similar passage 2 Thess. ii. 13.

through your entreaty] Same word as in *v.* 4. He is confident that they will pray for him and pray effectually.
Intercession on the human side, and supply of the Spirit
on the Divine side, secure his salvation. See on 1 Thess.
v. 25 ; 2 Thess. iii. 1 ; 2 Cor. i. 11. He believed intensely
in intercession.

and the consequent supply] The ' supply ' is bracketed
with ' your entreaty ' under one article, so that ' your '
belongs to both. The response to prayer is regarded as
certain and immediate ; Mk. xi. 24. The Philippians'
prayer ascends to heaven, and from heaven the supply
descends. It is doubtful whether ἐπιχορηγία means a
' bountiful supply ' or even an ' additional supply.' Language becomes weakened in course of time, and then addi-
tions are made to restore the original strength. Compounds
are often more common in late Greek than the simple
words. Thus ἐπιχορηγεῖν is used in much the same sense
as χορηγεῖν, and in N.T. it is more frequent. M. and M.,
Vocabulary, p. 251. So also ἀποθνήσκειν than θνήσκειν :
ἀποκτείνειν is frequent, while κτείνειν does not occur.

the Spirit of Jesus Christ] We need not ask whether this
means the Spirit which Jesus gives or the Spirit which He is.
St. Paul makes no hard and fast distinctions. See on 2 Cor.
iii. 17. See also Burton, *Spirit, Soul, and Flesh*, p. 190 ;
Headlam, *St. Paul and Christianity*, pp. 106 f. " It is, in fact,
impossible to make a rigid distinction in the Pauline Epistles
between the Holy Spirit and the Spiritual Christ. Life
in Christ and life in the Spirit are the same " (Gardner,
Religious Experience of St. Paul, p. 176).

20. intense anticipation] Or, ' eager expectation,' ' earnest
desire.' Ἀποκαραδοκία, which occurs elsewhere in Biblical
Greek, Rom. viii. 19 only, combines the ideas of turning

away from other objects (ἀπό) and stretching out the head
with eagerness to some one thing. The ἀπό might indicate
the *quarter whence* the thing desired is expected to come ;
or waiting *right on to the end*. In any case it implies fixedness.
Theodore makes the ἀπό negative, so that ἀποκαραδοκία =
τὸ ἀπελπίζειν = 'despair ' ; ' I am moved by despair and
help.' This can hardly be right. See Deissmann, *Light*, p.
377 ; Cremer, *Lex.* p. 177. Josephus says of himself
during the siege, that he disregarded those who were bringing
ladders, ἀπεκαραδόκει δὲ τὴν ὁρμὴν τῶν βελῶν, *BJ*. III.
vii. 26. Suicer, I. 451.

no atom of abject shame] With regard to the defence
and commendation of the Gospel. There will be no cowardly
reticence. Other possible failures, such as miscalculation
and disappointment, may be included in the comprehensive
ἐν οὐδενί which is balanced by the comprehensive ἐν πάσῃ
παρρησίᾳ.

every form of boldness of speech] The opposite of base
shame ; 1 Jn. ii. 28. See or: 2 Cor. iii. 12 and x. 8, and cf.
Eph. vi. 19.

the present crisis] His imprisonment and approaching
trial. His conviction is based on past and present experience.

Christ will be magnified] With characteristic humility
he does not say ' I will magnify Christ ' ; he claims no independent action, as if Christ were in his debt. Cf. μεγαλυν-
θῆναι, 2 Cor. x. 15.

in my person] Cf. 1 Cor. vi. 20 ; 2 Cor. iv. 10. His body
will be the sphere in which Christ's majesty will be made
conspicuous. It was his body that was in prison and
affliction.

whether . . . or] So that, whatever his enemies do to
him, they will promote the glory of *Christ*; not that,
as Jerome puts it, they cannot hurt *Paul*. Evidently this
is late in his imprisonment.

He has told the Philippians about his work and fellow-
workers ; he now goes on to tell them of his feelings

i. 21-26. THE APOSTLE'S PERPLEXITY AND HOPE.

²¹ For to me to live is Christ, and to die is gain. ²² But if I live in the flesh, this is the fruit of my labour : yet what I shall choose, I wot not. ²³ For I am in a strait betwixt two, having a desire to depart, and to be with Christ, which is far better. ²⁴ Nevertheless, to abide in the flesh, *is* more needful for you. ²⁵ And having this confidence, I know that I shall abide and continue with you all, for your furtherance and joy of faith, ²⁶ That your rejoicing may be more abundant in Jesus Christ for me, by my coming to you again.

We have here a third paradox ; this time an internal one, in the heart of the Apostle himself. He longs to die, and he longs to live. He yearns to depart, and be more closely with Christ ; and he yearns to stay, and do Christ's work among his beloved Philippians.

²¹ I am confident that He will be glorified by my life or my death, for, whatever it may be to others, to me life means Christ, and therefore death, which will take me to Him, means gain. ²² But if my life in the flesh thus far, if this has been fruitful of good work, and therefore may be equally fruitful in the future—then I do not decide what I am to choose ; ²³ but I am held in a strait between the two alternatives ; having my desire towards striking camp and being with Christ, for it is far, far better ; ²⁴ but to abide by the flesh is more necessary on account of you. ²⁵ And of this being fully confident, I know that I shall bide and abide here with all of you, to promote your advance in believing and your joy in believing, ²⁶ in order that your reason for boasting may, because of your relation to Christ Jesus, be more abundant in me, His Apostle, through my presence with you again.

21. **to me life means Christ**] The ' me ' is very emphatic. ' For *myself* there is no life worth calling life, except what is spent with Christ.' Not merely ' in my opinion,' but ' in my experience.' *Si vixero, Christo ;* or better, *Quicquid vivo, Christum vivo* (Bengel). Cf. iii. 8, 9 ; Gal. ii. 20. Not ' Christ is to me lyfe ' (Tindale), but ' to me living is Christ.'

death] ' Life ' means continuing to live, pres. infin., τὸ ζῆν. Note the change to the aor. infin., τὸ ἀποθανεῖν, ' to have died,' ' to be dead,' not τὸ ἀποθνήσκειν, ' the act of dying.' Cf. 2 Cor. vii. 3, εἰς τὸ συναποθανεῖν καὶ συνζῆν, ' to share life after death and before death with you.'

is gain] St. Paul is preparing for the statement in *v.* 23,

that for *him* to have left this life is preferable to being
in it. Of course he does not mean that only this life is
Christ, and that leaving this life (*i.e.* leaving Christ) is gain.
Cf. Wisd. iii. 1–3. Calvin remarks that this passage is fatal
to the view that the intermediate state is one of sleep and
unconsciousness.

22. **But if my life in the flesh**] The verse is [a well-
known *crux*, and certainty as to its exact interpretation
is impossible. The A.V. hardly does justice to the Greek.
The R.V. gives two renderings, one in the text, and one
in the margin. WH. margin suggests ἔργου καὶ τί
αἱρήσομαι; οὐ γνωρίζω. If . . . work, ' then what am I
to choose? I cannot say.' So also Blass, § 65, 1, § 77, 6.
Otherwise Winer, pp. 374, 751. In any case something
not in the Greek must be supplied, and ellipses are common
in Paul. The general meaning, however one may reach it,
is clear ; ' If my continuing to live in the flesh is to be
fruitful for the Gospel, I cannot declare what I am to
choose.' He adds ' in the flesh,' because ' death ' does not
mean ceasing to live ; for the same reason he substitutes
' striking camp ' for dying.

I do not decide] Or, ' I do not perceive,' ' I do not understand.' In classical Greek γνωρίζω means ' I *get* knowledge of,' or ' I *have* full knowledge of,' and this may be the
meaning here. But in N.T. the verb is commonly transi-
tive, ' I *make* known,' ' I declare ' ; 1 Cor. xii. 3, xv. 1 ;
2 Cor. viii. 1 ; Gal. i. 11 ; etc. ' I do not decide ' may
represent either use. See M. and M., p. 120.

23. **But I am held in a strait**] ' *For* I *am* in ' (A.V.) is a
false reading (γάρ for δέ) and an inadequate rendering of
συνέχομαι. The verb implies the pressure which confines
and restricts ; Lk. viii. 45 ; xii. 50, xix. 43 ; Acts xviii.
5. See on 2 Cor. v. 4, where συνέχει ἡμᾶς means ' hems us
in,' keeping us from all selfish motives. Cf. συνοχή, 2 Cor.
ii. 4.

between the two alternatives] ' From both the sides,'
ἐκ τῶν δυο, ' betwixt *the* two,' the two just mentioned.
As Seneca says (*Ep.* lxv. 18), *Sapiens assectatorque sapien-*

tiae adhaeret quidem in corpore suo, sed optima sui parte abest : et ita formatus est, ut illi nec amor vitae, nec odium sit. Patitur mortalia ; scit ampliora superesse. " To many of us life and death have seemed like two evils, and we knew not which was the less. To the Apostle they seem like two immense blessings, and he knows not which is the better." (Ad. Monod, quoted by Moule).

my desire towards] ' *The* desire,' the one which now consumes him and is decidedly in one direction.

striking camp] This is probably the metaphor by which ' to unloose ' ($\dot{a}\nu a\lambda\hat{v}\sigma a\iota$) comes to mean ' to depart from life.' M. and M., p. 36 ;·Burton, *Moods and Tenses*, § 107, 413. *Dissolvi* Vulg. represents the inferior reading $\dot{a}\nu a\lambda\nu-\theta\hat{\eta}\nu a\iota$. In inscriptions the verb is used of departing in death. Cf. 2 Cor. v. 1 ; 2 Tim. iv. 6 ; Clem. Rom. *Cor.* xliv. 5. Others suggest ' unloosing from moorings and setting sail ' as the metaphor. Tobit ii. 9 ; Judith xiii. 1 ; see Suicer.

being with Christ] Cf. 1 Thess. iv. 17. In both passages, as in Col. ii. 20, iii. 3, we have $\sigma\acute{v}\nu$, which implies closer union than $\mu\epsilon\tau\acute{a}$. Thackeray, *St. Paul and Jewish Thought*, pp. 128 f. The two infinitives have only one article ; departing and being with Christ are closely connected. Cf. ' To-day thou shalt be with me in Paradise,' Lk. xxiii. 43 ; also Acts vii. 59, words which St. Paul heard ; 2 Cor. v. 8. In 1 Thess. iv. 14, 16 and 1 Cor. xv. 51, 52 the dead are asleep and awake to be with Christ at His Return ; St. Paul has no fixed scheme of eschatology. Deissmann, *St. Paul*, p. 189.

far, far better] The comparative $\kappa\rho\epsilon\hat{i}\sigma\sigma o\nu$ is doubly strengthened with $\pi o\lambda\lambda\hat{\omega}\ \mu\hat{a}\lambda\lambda o\nu$, a combination unique in N.T. Cf. 2 Cor. iii. 9, vii. 13. Blass, § 44, 5. *Decedere est melius quam manere in carne : cum Christo esse, multo magis melius* (Bengel). Such strengthened comparatives occur in colloquial Latin. Plautus has *magis dulcius* and *magis certius*.

24. **to abide by the flesh**] Not ' *in* the flesh' (A.V., R.V.) ; the $\dot{\epsilon}\nu$ is an interpolation from *v.* 22. Except in the

strictly local sense, as ' in Ephesus,' 1 Cor. xvi. 8, St. Paul never has ἐν after ἐπιμένειν. ' To abide by ' means ' to retain with all its consequences.' ' Nevertheless ' (A.V.) is too strong for δέ.

more necessary] There is more obligation to adopt this alternative. Cf. St. Paul's speech, Acts xiii. 46.

on account of you] Or, ' for your sake,' δι᾽ ὑμᾶς. He has no weak longing for death as an escape from the work and worry of this world. *Nam ipse vitae plenus est, cui adjici nihil desiderat sua causa, sed eorum quibus utilis est. Liberaliter facit, quod vivit. . . . Dolorem fert, mortem expectat* (Seneca, *Ep.* xcviii. 15, 17). Wetstein quotes *Ingentis animi est aliena causa ad vitam reverti : quod magni viri saep fecerunt* (*Ep.* civ. 4).

25. of this being fully confident] He is not claiming to have had a divine revelation to this effect ; he is giving his own conviction. He said that he *knew* (οἶδα there as here) that the Ephesians would never see him again (Acts xx. 25) ; yet he did return to Ephesus (2 Tim. i. 15, 18, iv. 20). *Nihil nisi sub conditione sperat* (Calvin). For πέποιθα see on *v.* 6.

bide and abide with] Μενῶ καὶ παραμενῶ. The latter means ' remain beside,' ' continue with.' The verb often implies a voluntary remaining when one might depart. For similar playing on words see on iii. 3 ; 2 Thess. iii. 11 ; 2 Cor. i. 13, iv. 8, etc. This is some indication that he expects his trial to take place soon, and therefore that he had already been imprisoned for a long time.

all of you] He once more (see on *v.* 8) intimates that all his Philippian converts are included. It is not likely that all his converts everywhere are meant.

advance in believing] ' Advance ' and ' joy ' have only one article (see on *v.* 19), and therefore ' in believing ' (τῆς πίστεως) belongs to both. See on *v.* 12 for ' advance.' ' Joy,' the dominant note, sounds once more.

26. reason for boasting] Cf. Ecclus. ix. 16. The sentence is somewhat obscure ; but ἐν Χριστῷ ᾽Ιησοῦ belongs to περισσεύῃ, not to καύχημα, for which A.V. wrongly has ' rejoicing ' here, ii. 16 and iii. 3.

presence with you again] Or, ' my coming to visit you again ' ; cf. ii. 12 ; 1 Cor. xvi. 17 ; 2 Cor. x. 10.* This meaning of παρουσία is common in papyri. The idea of ' coming in state,' or ' paying an official visit,' which the word sometimes implies, is probably absent here. See on 1 Thess. ii. 19. Meanwhile, until he can come, he sends exhortations and instructions.

i. 27-ii. 18.   HORTATORY AND DOCTRINAL

This portion of the Epistle falls easily into three distinct paragraphs, which, however, are closely connected with one another, the doctrinal part forming a link between the two exhortations, both of which are directed to the same end, viz., the promotion of unity by the practice of self-suppression. Evidently there had been at Philippi rivalries and disputes, if not something more serious. This was a real drawback to the Apostle's general satisfaction, and he now begins to deal with it. We have i. 27-ii. 4 Exhortation to Unity and Self-negation ; ii. 5–11 Christ the great Example of Self-negation and Humility ; and ii. 12–18 Further Exhortation to Unity and Submission. As before, it is convenient to break up the long Greek sentences.

i. 27–ii. 4.   EXHORTATION TO UNITY AND SELF-NEGATION.

[27] Only let your conversation be as it becometh the Gospel of Christ, that whether I come and see you, or else be absent, I may hear of your affairs, that ye stand fast in one spirit, with one mind, striving together for the faith of the Gospel, [28] And in nothing terrified by your adversaries : which is to them an evident token of perdition, but to you of salvation, and that of God. [29] For unto you it is given in the behalf of Christ, not only to believe on him, but also to suffer for his sake, [30] Having the same conflict which ye saw in me, and now hear *to be* in me.

ii. [1] If *there be* therefore any consolation in Christ, if any comfort of love, if any fellowship of the Spirit, if any bowels and mercies, [2] Fulfil ye my joy, that ye be likeminded, having the same love,

---

* If this letter had been written at Caesarea, he would be expecting to visit, not Philippi, but Rome, to which he had appealed.

being of one accord, of one mind.   ³ Let nothing be *done* through strife, or vainglory, but in lowliness of mind let each esteem other better than themselves.   ⁴ Look not every man on his own things, but every man also on the things of others.

We have the usual alternation of subject.   Having for a while spoken of himself, he now turns again to his converts.

²⁷ Only, whatever happens to me, do remember of what Kingdom you are citizens, and do live worthily of the Gospel of Christ.   So that whether I come and see you with my own eyes, or stay away and hear all about you from others, let me have the joy of knowing that you are standing firm in one and the same spirit, with one soul fighting side by side in alliance with the Faith of the Gospel.   ²⁸ And never be scared by any assault made upon you by those who oppose you.   Fearlessness of this kind is a clear intimation to them of their perdition, but of your salvation.   And the fearlessness with its meaning comes of course from God ;   ²⁹ because on you there was conferred by Him the privilege that on Christ's behalf you should not only in faith surrender to Him, but also on His behalf suffer.   ³⁰ For you have entered the same sort of arena of conflict in which you saw me contending at Philippi and now hear of my contending in Rome.

ii. ¹ It is therefore to your own experience that I can appeal.   If your life in Christ has any power to persuade you, if love supplies any encouragement, if fellowship with the Spirit of love is a reality, if you feel any tenderness and compassion, ² complete in me the joy which you have already inspired.   You can do this by being of the same mind among yourselves, by mutual and impartial love, by being knit together in soul, by being of one mind.   ³ Do nothing under the influence of partisanship, nothing under the influence of personal vanity ;   on the contrary, with lowliness of mind, each of you regarding one another to be superior to himself, ⁴ each and all of you adopting as your aim, not your own interests alone, but beyond them the interests of others.

27. whatever happens to me] This is implied in the ' only ' (μόνον).   For a similar ellipse after μόνον see Gal. ii. 10, vi. 12.   In 2 Thess. ii. 7 there is probably no ellipse.   What follows here is very emphatic.

of what Kingdom you are citizens] Πολιτεύεσθε implies ' behaving as citizens ' (R.V. margin), and in iii. 20 the Philippians are reminded that ' our citizenship (πολίτευμα) is by its very nature (ὑπάρχει) in heaven.'   The expression ἀξίως πολιτευόμενοι is used by Clement of Rome *Cor.*

xxi. 1 ; cf. xxi. 1, liv. 4.   The verb is no doubt purposely
substituted for the more usual περιπατεῖν to remind the
Philippians that they are fellow-citizens and ought to be
united.   Philippi was a Roman colony, and the idea of
citizenship would be readily appreciated there.   Elsewhere
in N.T. the verb occurs only in Acts xxiii. 1, in a speech
of St. Paul.   Cf. 2 Macc. vi. 1, xi. 25, and see Suicer, II. 799.

worthily of] Cf. 1 Thess. ii. 12 ; Rom. xvi. 2 ; Eph. iv. 1 ;
i. 10.   Deissmann, *Bible Studies*, pp. 248 f.

whether . . . or] The construction is not quite smooth,
but the meaning is plain.

all about you] With τὰ περὶ ὑμῶν here and ii. 19, 20, cf.
τὰ περὶ ἡμῶν, Eph. vi. 22.

are standing firm] The present of the strong form στήκω is
used, as in 2 Thess. ii. 15 and Gal. v. 1, followed by ἐν, as in
iv. 1 ; 1 Thess. iii. 8 ; 1 Cor. xvi. 13.   Kennedy, *Sources of
N.T. Grk.* p. 158.   The thought of contests in the arena
seems to be in the Apostle's mind throughout the passage ;
cf. *v.* 30 ; ii. 16, iii. 14.   While our Lord's illustrations are
mostly from external nature and country life, those of His
Apostle are mostly from city life—the stadium, the army,
slavery, legal institutions, trade, etc.   Conybeare and
Howson, ch. xx. *sub init.*   E. A. Abbott, *The Fourfold Gospel*,
V. p. 236.

in one and the same spirit] P. Ewald takes ἐν ἑνὶ πνεύματι
to mean the Holy Spirit, comparing Eph. i. 17, iv. 3 ; so also
Moule, comparing 1 Cor. xii. 13 ; Eph. ii. 18.

with one soul] Cf. Acts iv. 32.   The best ancient Versions
and Chrysostom connect ' with one soul ' with ' stand firm.'
The emphatic position before ' fighting side by side with '
is more forcible.   On ψυχή see Hatch, *Biblical Greek*, pp.
101–109.

in alliance with the Faith] This rather than ' for the faith '
(A.V., R.V.) seems to be the meaning ; but ' shoulder
to shoulder *with one another* ' may be right.   This, however,
is already expressed by ' with one soul.'

' The Faith ' is personified, as the Truth is in 1 Cor. xiii.
6.   In any conflict, Christians must range themselves

on its side. The Faith of the Gospel is that which Christians have to believe and practise. Harnack, *Dogmengeschichte*, I. pp. 129 ff.

28. **never be scared**] Πτύρομαι occurs nowhere else in Scripture. It is used of animals shying when startled, and often figuratively. The opponents are Jews or heathen, and this is one o several indications that Christians in Philippi and elsewhere in Macedonia were suffering persecution. See on i. Cor. xvi. 9 and 2 Cor. vii. 5.

of this kind] 'Of such a character as to be.' The pronoun ἥτις is attracted into the gender of ἔνδειξις, 'intimation,' or 'demonstration.' This word is Pauline in N.T. (Rom. iii. 25, 26 ; 2 Cor. viii. 24), and it is not found in LXX. It means an appeal to facts. For the attraction cf. Eph. iii. 13.

their perdition] The fearlessness of the Christian athlete shows his opponents that they are contending against something more than human force. If they kill him, they send him to the eternal joy which he desires, while they make their own entrance into it less possible. St. Paul nowhere defines 'perdition,' which is the opposite of 'salvation.' Cf. iii. 19.

your salvation] In complete generality of meaning. See Hort on σωτηρίαν ψυχῶν, 1 Pet. i. 9. 'To you of salvation' (A.V.) is an inferior reading, ὑμῖν for ὑμῶν. The pronoun is emphatic here and in the next verse.

the fearlessness with its meaning] This is included in the neuter τοῦτο. It is owing to Divine agency that the Christian athlete is free from fear, and that this fact has its twofold message, whether the world recognizes this or not. This twofold message is a 'cloud and darkness' to the adversaries, but 'light by night' to those whom they persecute (Barry).

29. **because on you**] How does the Apostle know that this comes from God ? Because an immense privilege and honour has been conferred on his converts, which would be unintelligible otheiwise. *Gratiae munus signum salutis* (Bengel). The verb ἐχαρίσθη implies this ; it was a free

gift, and an invaluable one ; Lk. vii. 21, 42.   Cf. ἡ χάρις, i. 7, and ἐχαρίσατο, ii. 9.

on Christ's behalf] We have this repeated for emphasis, and between we have the surrender to Him ; τὸ ὑπὲρ . . . τὸ εἰς . . . τὸ ὑπέρ.   Evidently ' to suffer ' was to have come after ' on Christ's behalf.'   But it adds point to insert the free gift of faith as the first step in the high privilege, and the ' suffer ' comes with emphasis at the close. ' Given (or granted) in the behalf of Christ ' (A.V., R.V.) is not the right connexion.

not only] For οὐ μόνον see Burton, § 481.

in faith surrender to Him] Εἰς αὐτὸν πιστεύειν is frequent in John : elsewhere in Paul, Rom. x. 14 and Gal. ii. 16 only.

We see here the boldness and sureness of St. Paul.   Christian courage must come from God, because, after enabling us to put our whole trust in Christ, He grants the glory of suffering for Christ.   See on 2 Cor. xii. 10 ; also F. B. Westcott, *St. Paul and Justification*, pp. 307 f.   To the pagan this is absurd paradox ; he does not wish to suffer at all.   But Christian experience proves that the paradox is true ; Acts v. 41 ; Rom. v. 3 ; Col. i. 24.   Πιστεύειν εἰς is the most common formula for absolute trust with regard to Christ or God.

30. **the same sort of arena of conflict**] Cf. 1 Tim. vi. 12 ; 2 Tim. iv. 7.   In 1 Thess. ii. 2 he alludes, as here, to what he had suffered from the Jewish mob and the Roman duumvirs at Philippi.   The nominative participle (τὸν αὐτὸν ἀγῶνα ἔχοντες), though not strictly grammatical, for it looks back to ὑμῖν, is very natural, especially when we remember that St. Paul was dictating.   Moulton, *Prolegomena*, p. 225.   Cf. ἀνεχόμενοι, Eph. iv. 2.   It is not necessary, in order to save the grammar, to make ἥτις . . . πάσχειν a long parenthesis.   Note οἷον, not ὅν : it was not identical, for the Philippians were not in prison ; but they were exposed to persecution.*

* That " some of the Christians were in the custody of the military authorities as seditious persons " at Philippi at this time is rather more than can safely be inferred from this passage.

now hear] From Epaphroditus, or whoever read this letter to them.

ii. 1. in Christ] See on i. 13. The four clauses seem to be arranged in pairs, one relating to union with Christ and its benefit, the other to communion with the Spirit and its benefit.

any power to persuade you] The context shows that παρα-κλῆσις here means 'exhortation' rather than 'supplication' or 'consolation' (Vulg.). Cf. 1 Cor. xiv. 3 ; 2 Cor. viii. 17).

encouragement] With παρακλῆσις and παραμύθιον (Wisd. iii. 18) cf. παρακαλοῦντες and παραμυθούμενοι (1 Thess. ii. 12).

fellowship with the Spirit] κοινωνία (i. 5, iii. 10), συνκοι-νωνός (i. 7) and κοινωνεῖν (iv. 15) are characteristic words in this letter, which pleads for unity, and the renderings ought to harmonize. This passage decides for 'fellowship.' See Robertson and Plummer on 1 Cor. x. 16 and cf. 2 Cor. xiii. 13.

tenderness] Σπλάγχνα as in i. 8 ; and the word for 'compassion' is also plural, οἰκτιρμοί. In Scripture both words are commonly plural. In N.T. οἰκτιρμοῦ, Col. iii. 12, is the sole exception. It is extraordinary that these plurals, according to overwhelming evidence, are preceded, like κοινωνία, by εἴ τις. St. Paul, in dictating, probably said εἴ τις, meaning to use another singular noun ; and then used two plurals, as best expressing his meaning. Scrivener, *Introd.* II. p. 386 ; Moulton, *Proleg.* p. 59 ; A. T. Robertson, *Gr.* p. 410. On the fondness of St. Paul for long enumera-tions of cognate moral qualities see Simcox, *Writers of the N.T.* pp. 35 f. Chrysostom calls attention to the intense earnestness of these four clauses. The need of unity is so great that exhortation has become entreaty.

2. complete in me the joy] Already mentioned in i. 4, 5. We have here the same verb as in Jn. iii. 29, 'This my joy has been made complete,' πεπλήρωται : also 1 Jn. i. 4 ; 2 Jn. 12.

being of the same mind] He has prayer for *all* of them

(i. 4), he thinks well of them *all* (i. 7), they *all* share grace
with him (i. 7), he yearns after *all* of them (i. 8). He has
begged them to be united in fighting on the side of the
Faith (i. 27). Here, in the " tautology of earnestness," he
enlarges on the great need for united thought and action.
For ἵνα see Burton, § 215, 217 ; Lightfoot on Col. i. 9 ;
for τὸ αὐτὸ φρ., Deissmann, *B.S.* p. 256.

by mutual and impartial love] So that the love may be
' the same ' in all relations. There is such a thing as
unity in hatred.

knit together in soul] Σύνψυχοι occurs nowhere else in
N.T. The classical word is σύμφρων. It is better to have
a comma after σύνψυχοι, rather than make it coalesce with
τὸ ἓν φρονοῦντες, ' with according soul being of one mind.'
We have four antecedents with ' if ' in *v.* 1, and four conse-
quents in *v.* 2.

being of one mind] He finds it difficult to explain without
repetition ; cf. iv. 1. He ends where he started, slightly
varying the expression, by substituting ' the one,' τὸ ἕν,
for ' the same,' τὸ αὐτό. He has his favourite verb φρονεῖν
with both ; and it always refers, not to any particular
opinion, but to a permanent view or feeling. ' Minding
the one thing needful ' is a possible meaning. But cf.
the current phrase ἕν καὶ τ'αὐτό, *unum atque idem*,
' one and the same.' There is similar repetition iii. 7–9 and
iv. 12.

3. **Do nothing, etc.**] ' Do ' is not expressed here, any more
than in the proverbial μηδὲν ἄγαν. Cf. μὴ παιδὶ μάχαιραν, μὴ
πῦρ ἐπὶ πῦρ. Ignatius, *Philad.* viii. 2 has μηδὲν κατ' ἐριθείαν
πράσσετε. But it is perhaps simpler to supply φρονοῦντες
from the previous clause ; ' *having in mind* nothing in
the way of partisanship.' The meaning is much the same.
For ἐριθεία see on i. 17.

personal vanity] As opposed to zeal for the glory of God.
Personal vanity and strife are often cause and effect, setting
oneself up provokes others to pull one down. Κενοδοξία
has this meaning here, as in Macc. ii. 15, viii. 18 ; also
in Philo and Polybius. But in Wisd. xiv. 14 it seems

The language of the passage is carefully chosen, with balances and rhythmical clauses. The Apostle "loves that rhythm of style for which his taste had been sharpened by the language of the Prophets. Whole sections of his Epistles can be divided into short complete lines like poetry in prose " (Von Soden, p. 25). A. S. Way makes this passage into a " Hymn of the Incarnation." See on 1 Thess. iv. 17, p. 78 footnote. See also Deissmann's excellent remarks, *St. Paul*, pp. 168 f. ; Headlam, *St. Paul and Christianity*, pp. 58 f. ; Moffatt, *Intr. to the Literature of the N.T.* pp. 57, 167 ; Ramsay, *The First Christian Century*, pp. 105 f. ; Rostron, *Christology*, pp. 112–129.

[5] Reflect in your own minds this, which was also the thought in the mind of Christ Jesus ; [6] who, though He was by nature in the form of God, yet did not regard being on an equality with God as a prize to be strenuously secured. [7] On the contrary, of His own free will He divested Himself of His glory in assuming the form of a bondservant by being born in human guise. [8] And being recognized by men as a man in all that is external, He humbled Himself by becoming obedient to God, which extended to submission unto death, and not merely death, but death on the cross. [9] Therefore in consequence of this God supremely exalted Him, and conferred upon Him the name which is above every name, [10] so that in Jesus' Name every knee should bow, of beings in heaven, and beings on earth, and beings under the earth, [11] and every tongue freely confess that Jesus Christ is Lord, and all this to promote the glory of God the Father.

5. Reflect in your own minds] He continues to dwell on the condition of their minds ; φρονεῖν, as twice in *v.* 2.

the thought in the mind] All that the Greek gives is ' which also in Christ Jesus,' and the meaning almost certainly is ' Think in yourselves that which He also thought in Himself,' understanding ἐφρονήθη : ' Model your thoughts on His. It is sometimes understood to mean, ' Cultivate the same unity among yourselves *as you have enjoyed in relation to*

fait taire la raison, et rend la foi même raisonnable (Massillon). *Qu'est-ce qu'être membre de Jésus-Christ ? C'est suivre la destinée du chef, et lui être conforme ; mourir à tout avec lui ; ne former au dedans de soi que ses desires et ses sentiments ; ne pas chercher sa consolation en ce monde comme lui (ibid.)*

E

Christ.' What follows about Christ as a pattern of humility
and self-renunciation is decisive against this. The Latin
of Theodore of Mopsuestia has *Talia sapite et qualia Christus
videtur sapuisse :* Beza *Is sit affectus in vobis, qui fuit et in
Christo.* Bossuet *Entrons dans les mêmes dispositions où a
été le Seigneur Jésus.*

The next two verses (6, 7) are among the most difficult
passages in Scripture. Each clause is open to more than
one interpretation, and it is impossible to be certain about
the correctness of the several solutions which one decides to
adopt. The leading words in most of the clauses are of
disputed, if not doubtful, meaning. Note the three verbs
which express existence; εἶναι ' to be,' ὑπάρχειν ' to be
essentially,' γίνεσθαι ' to come to be,' ' to become.'

6. though He was by nature] Or, ' being originally ' (R.V.
margin) : not ὤν (i. 1 ; Rom. i 7 ; 1 Cor. i. 2 ; etc.), but
ὑπάρχων (see Evans on 1 Cor. xi. 7). The word points
clearly to the pre-existence of Christ, to the period prior
to the Incarnation. The participle is probably imperfect ;
and the expression points clearly to the meaning of the
words which accompany it. Sabatier calls the four words
" the most exalted metaphysical definition ever given
by Paul to the Person of Christ " (*The Apostle Paul,*
p. 259).

"The epistle sets forth three different states of the Messiah :
pre-existence in heaven, humiliation on earth, and enthrone-
ment in heaven. Each of these is presented with a wealth
of meaning beyond anything taught in the previous Paulinism " (C. A. Briggs, *The Messiah of the Apostles,* p. 179).

in the form of God] Ἐν μορφῇ Θεοῦ. The best alternative
for ' form ' here is ' nature,'—that which He was really.
But ' by nature ' being implied in ὑπάρχων the more literal
' form ' is the better rendering. ' In the form of God ' means
' possessing the Divine attributes.' Cf. the ' image (εἰκών)
of God,' 2 Cor. iv. 4 ; Col. i. 15, 16 ; and ' the expression of
His essence ' (χαρακτὴρ τῆς ὑποστάσεως αὐτοῦ) Heb. i. 3—
phrases which come near to the Johannine doctrine of the
Λόγος. See Lightfoot on Col. iii. 10, J. H. Bernard on 2

Cor. iv. 4, Westcott on Heb. i. 3, Pullan, *Early Christian Doctrine*, p. 21, and *Foundations*, pp. 192 f.

did not regard] The same verb as in *v.* 4, perhaps purposely repeated.

being on an equality] We have here, not ἴσον τῷ Θεῷ, as Jn. v. 18, but ἴσα Θεῷ, which *possibly* implies the Divine prerogatives rather than the Divine Person, ' the being equal things with God,' or perhaps ' existence on equality with God.'

a prize to be strenuously secured] The meaning of ἁρπαγμός remains open to doubt, but the idea of ' robbery ' or ' plundering ' may be set aside. The Latin rendering *rapina* has misled many translators and commentators. Nor need the original distinction, between ἁρπαγμός, the ' process or act of plundering,' and ἅρπαγμα, a ' piece of plunder,' be maintained. In late Greek the differences implied by differences of termination become blurred ; *e.g.* θεσμός and ἱλασμός represent a result rather than a process or act ; and the difference between βρῶσις and βρῶμα, πόσις and πόμα is sometimes ignored ; Theodore here treats ἁρπαγμός as the same as ἅρπαγμα. It means ' a catch,' something which is of great value, perhaps without the original idea of acquisition. The latter point is in dispute. Does ἁρπαγμός mean a treasure to be eagerly acquired, or a treasure to be tenaciously retained ? The word may seem to imply the former and the context is not decisive. On the one hand it is said that, if Christ was already by nature in the form of God, possessing all the Divine attributes, how could He regard equality with God as a treasure to be *acquired* ? On the other hand, by becoming incarnate, He treated it as a treasure which He would not *jealously cling to and hold fast.* ' Secure ' covers either meaning, ' acquire ' or ' retain.' If ' acquire ' is preferred, we may interpret that He might (as He was tempted to do) have used His Divine powers in such a way as to force men to recognize Him as the Son of God, ' making Himself equal to God ' ; and this He refused to do ; τὴν ἀξίαν ἐκείνην ἀπέκρυψεν (Theodore), *Quod erat, humilitate celavit* (Pelagius). But we cannot decide by principles of logic matters which transcend human reason. It is possible that St. Paul is here using language of the pre-existence of Christ which logically is appropriate to the incarnate Son.

There is no need to suppose that he is thinking of the First Adam, who was tempted to become as God (Gen. iii. 5), or of the fall of Lucifer (Is. xiv. 12–17).

7. **on the contrary**] So far from regarding the Divine attributes as something to be carefully secured, He voluntarily let them go. This seems to be the main feature in the Example, readiness to surrender what was rightly His own.

divested Himself of His glory] Cf. 2 Cor. viii. 9. Two features in Christ are singled out for imitation, His self-negation and His humility ; the former is mentioned here. ' Himself ' is emphatic by position (ἑαυτὸν ἐκένωσεν) intimating that it was His own doing. Cf. μὴ τὰ ἑαυτῶν, v. 4. ' Made Himself of no reputation ' (A.V.) is very inadequate : *semet ipsum exinanivit* (Vulg.) is better. Sanday, *The Oracles of God*, p. xiv.*

It does not help us to say that ' He emptied Himself ' is a sentence complete in itself, and requires no secondary object. A secondary object must be understood. He emptied Himself *of* something. A reservoir cannot empty itself without parting with its contents, and the contents in this case are the glories of the Divine nature. *The exact meaning of this is beyond us.* Attempts to explain the union of Godhead and manhood are inevitably failures. " Any attempt to commit Paul to a precise theological state-

---

* See Milton's Ode on the Nativity, i. 2.
    " That glorious Form, that light insufferable,
        *   *   *   *   *   *
    He laid aside : and here with us to be,
    Forsook the courts of everlasting day,
    And chose with us a darksome house of mortal clay."
In Westcott's words, it was " a laying aside of the mode of divine existence " (on Jn. i. 14). The whole note is illuminating. " The Indwelling of the pleroma refers to the Eternal Word, and not to the incarnate Christ " (Lightfoot on Col. ii. 9).

ment of the limitations of Christ's humanity involves the reader in a hopeless maze. . . . Christ's consciousness of deity was not suspended during His earthly life. He knew that He had glory with the Father before the world was, and would receive it back " (Vincent, p. 89). On the other hand, "He lived according to the conditions of man's life, and died under the circumstances of man's mortality " (Westcott on Heb. ii. 18). The emptying is described as a climax ; *status exinanitionis gradatim pro-fundior* (Bengel).

in assuming the form of a bondservant] A complete anti-thesis to the ' form of God ' ; we have μορφή in both places, and therefore the same English word in both. Here one would prefer ' nature,' because ' form ' might suggest that He merely *looked* like a bondservant, that He was *disguised* as one ; which is utterly misleading. Against this gross misinterpretation of St. Paul's language Gregory Nazianzen protests in his letter against Apollinarius (*Ep*. cii.). Just as before the Incarnation He was really and essentially Θεός, so at the Incarnation He became really and essentially δοῦλος. The λαβών emphasizes the voluntariness of the change. It was not imposed upon Him ; He assumed it ; and the two aorists show that the emptying and the assuming were contemporaneous. They give two aspects of the same act.*

To whom was He a bondservant ? To God, whose will was His will, and perhaps we may say to the whole race of mankind. But in Mk. x. 45 and Lk. xxii. 27 we have διακονεῖν. Christ ' ministered ' to many individuals, but we are nowhere told that He was the ' bondservant ' of any human being. Nor is the Suffering Servant in Isaiah in the Apostle's thought ; that is always παῖς, not δοῦλος.

---

* *Sa puissance se change en faiblesse ; sa sagesse infinie n'est plus qu'une raison, naissante et envelloppée ; son immensité parait ren-fermée dans les bornes d'un corps mortel ; l'image de la substance de son Père est cachée sous la vile forme d'esclave ; son éternelle origine commence à compter des temps et des moments ; enfin, it parail anéanti dans tous ses titres* (Massillon).

being born in human guise] 'Being born' (γενόμενος), like 'assuming,' is in contrast to what He 'was by nature' (ὑπάρχων) ; and 'guise' or 'similitude' (ὁμοίωμα) is in contrast to 'form' or 'essence' (μορφή). Therefore the noun implies the reality of the likeness rather than the reality of the human nature (Trench, *Syn.* § xv.). The latter has been stated in the previous clause. There was " substantial likeness " (F. B. Westcott, *St. Paul and Justification*, pp. 242, 291). We are concerned now with what was external and apparent. Elsewhere St. Paul insists again and again on the reality of Christ's Humanity ; iii. 10 ; Rom. viii. 3 ; Gal. iv. 4 ; Col. i. 22, 24 ; etc. 'In human guise,' not merely in the likeness of a man (cf. Mt. xiii. 52), but 'of men' (ἀνθρώπων), of the whole human race, to whom He seemed to be one of themselves. He was really such (Heb. ii. 17), but He was a great deal more.

8. **being recognized**] 'Found' (εὑρεθείς) expresses the quality, not as it exists in itself, but as it is perceived and recognized ; iii. 9 ; 1 Cor. iv. 2 ; 2 Cor. v. 3, xi. 12.

in all that is external] In popular language σχῆμα and μορφή are as convertible as 'shape' and 'form' are in English ; but in technical language σχῆμα indicates what is external and changeable, μορφή what is essential and permanent. This distinction prevails in N.T. in the use of the two words and of the derivatives of each ; μετασχηματίζε-σθαι, συνσχηματίζεσθαι, μεταμορφοῦσθαι, συμμορφοῦσθαι (iii. 10), σύμμορφος (iii. 21), μορφοῦσθαι, μόρφωσις. The meanings in this passage are clear. They "imply respectively the true Divine nature of our Lord (μορφὴ Θεοῦ), the true human nature (μορφὴ δούλου), and the externals of the human nature (σχήματι ὡς ἄνθρωπος)." Lightfoot, p. 133.

For σχήματι the Latin Versions have *figura, habitu, specie.* Whereas μορφή can be used of both Godhead and manhood, σχῆμα is applicable to the latter only. Cf. 1 Cor. vii. 31, where σχῆμα is used of the external world. In Christian interpolations in the Testaments of the XII Patriarchs we have both terms used of the manhood ; *Zabulon* ix. 8

ὄψεσθε Θεὸν ἐν σχήματι ἀνθρώπου, and *Benjamin* x. 7 ἐπὶ γῆς φανέντα ἐν μορφῇ ἀνθρώπου. But possibly both terms may be meant to refer to the externals.

He humbled Himself] The change of order is significant : ἑαυτὸν ἐκένωσεν, 'He emptied *Himself* '; ἐταπείνωσεν ἑαυτόν, 'He *humbled* Himself.' Even as man He humbled Himself to the uttermost.

obedient to God] *Obedientia servum decet* (Bengel) ; ' to God ' is implied in *v.* 9. He became so by a life of absolutely perfect obedience in all things, Heb. v. 8. ' Obedient unto death ' (A.V.) is misleading, as if the obedience was rendered to Death : *oboediens usque ad mortem* (Vulg.) is the meaning. And He *became* obedient by *learning* to be so through the things which He suffered (Heb. v. 8).

which included] which went as far as that, μέχρι θανάτου, Heb. xii. 4 ; 2 Macc. xiii. 14.

and not merely death] This is implied in δέ. The prayers in Gethsemane may be in St. Paul's mind. Crucifixion was a death of extreme suffering and shame ; being nailed to a tree like vermin. Christ had assumed the nature of a slave to God ; and crucifixion was the death of a slave to man (Gal. v. 11 ; Heb. xii. 2), a death excruciating and accursed (Gal. iii. 13). The Apostle may be suggesting that, willing as he was to share his Master's sufferings and death, yet as a Roman citizen he could not be crucified, and members of the Roman colony at Philippi would appreciate this privilege and privation. Cicero, *Pro Rabirio* v. 10, points out how impossible such a death was for a Roman.

Some critics divide *vv.* 6–8 into four clauses, which seem to be balanced by four corresponding clauses in *vv.* 9–11. Thus, (1) ὃς ἐν μορφῇ . . . (2) ἀλλά . . . (3) ἐν ὁμοιώματι . . . (4) ἐταπείνωσεν . . . (1) διὸ καὶ . . . (2) καὶ ἐχαρίσατο . . . (3) ἵνα ἐν τῷ ὀνόματι . . . (4) καὶ πᾶσα. See J. Weiss in *Theologische Studien*, Göttingen, 1897, pp. 190 f.

9. Therefore in consequence of this] Διὸ καί. The καί implies that God *on His side responds*, in accordance with the principle that he who humbles himself is exalted ; Mt. xxiii. 12 ; Lk. xiv. 11, xviii. 14 ; cf. Jas. iv. 6 ; 1 Pet. v. 5.

' Him ' is emphatic by position, as is natural in a statement of reciprocity ; He emptied *Himself*, and God exalted *Him*.

supremely exalted Him] Αὐτὸν ὑπερύψωσεν. On St. Paul's fondness for words compounded with ὑπέρ see on 2 Thess. i. 3. This more than cancels the emptying and humiliating. Cf. Ps. xcvi. (xcvii.) 9.

conferred] See on i. 29 and Hort on 1 Pet. i. 21.

the Name] Not ' *a* Name ' (A.V.) ; τὸ ὄνομα is the right reading, and ' the Name ' is probably ' Lord,' as the equivalent of ' Jehovah ' in O.T. See on i. 2.*

It is not quite certain that any name is meant. ' Name ' may mean ' rank ' or ' dignity.' This makes excellent sense here, and to some seems to be preferable. God gave Him the dignity which is above every dignity.

above every name] *Non modo super omne nomen humanum* (Bengel).

10. **in Jesus' Name**] Not ' at ' (A.V.) ; Ps. lxiii. 4. ' The Name which belongs to Jesus ' is the meaning ; that which represents His majesty in its completeness, far above the designation of any created being (Eph. i. 21). Theodoret thinks that ' Son of God ' or ' God ' is the name. Some moderns decide for ' Jesus ' ; *e.g.* Case, *Evolution of Early Christianity*, p. 158. But ' the Name ' in *v.* 10 must mean the same as in *v.* 9, and in *v.* 9 ' Jesus ' cannot be meant, for many persons have been called ' Jesus,' and Christ Himself had the name of Jesus during His earthly life, before the extremity of an accursed death. The passage is often strangely misunderstood, as ordering the custom of bowing the head when the name of Jesus is mentioned. ' Bending the knee ' is often a metaphor for reverence and worship or prayer ; Rom. xi. 4 ; Eph. iii. 14. " To bow the knee in the name of Jesus is to pay adoration in that sphere of author-ity, grace, and glory for which the name stands " (Vincent). However we may explain the details, the meaning is that

* " What name is meant is clear from the fact that because of this name He becomes the object of the adoration of all. For they all are to confess that Jesus Christ is the divine Lord in the sense in which God alone bears this name " (B. Weiss).

every being should pay the utmost respect to the majesty of the incarnate and glorified Son. See Is. xlv. 23 which is adapted here and quoted Rom. xiv. 11 ; also 1 Pet. iii. 22.

in heaven and on earth] Whether the adjectives are masculine or neuter, the triplet is an expansion of ' the whole creation,' ' all the works of the Lord.' Cf. Rev. v. 13, where ' and on the sea ' is added. Wiclif (*De Benedicta Incarnacione,* iii.) has *omne genu flectatur celestium, quos restituit, terrestrium, quos redemit, et infernorum, quos spoliavit.* But respecting the three classes " we know too little of the Apostle's ideas to be able to venture upon a decision " (P. Ewald). See M. and M., *Vocabulary,* pp. 236, 252.

11. **freely confess**] Or, ' joyfully proclaim.' All that ἐξομολογεῖσθαι of necessity means is ' openly declare '; but LXX usage gives the verb the notion of praise or thanksgiving, and that idea is very appropriate here. M. and M., *Vocabulary,* p. 224. Cf. Rom. xv. 9 ; 1 Cor. xii. 3. Acts viii. 37 cannot be quoted as part of the true text.

is Lord] Emphatic by position.

and all this] ' To the glory etc.' need not be restricted to *v.* 11 : it probably looks back to *vv.* 9 and 10. " Wherever the Son is glorified, the Father is glorified " (Chrysostom).

ii. 12–18. FURTHER EXHORTATION TO UNITY AND SUBMISSION.

¹² Wherefore, my beloved, as ye have always obeyed, not as in my presence only, but now much more in my absence ; work out your own salvation with fear, and trembling. ¹³ For it is God which worketh in you, both to will and to do, of *his* good pleasure. ¹⁴ Do all things without murmurings, and disputings : ¹⁵ That ye may be blameless and harmless, the sons of God, without rebuke, in the midst of a crooked and perverse nation, among whom ye shine as lights in the world : ¹⁶ Holding forth the word of life, that I may rejoice in the day of Christ, that I have not run in vain, neither laboured in vain. ¹⁷ Yea, and if I be offered upon the sacrifice and service of your faith, I joy and rejoice with you all. ¹⁸ For the same cause also do ye joy, and rejoice with me.

The Apostle proceeds to press home the lesson of Christ's

self-negation, humility, and obedience. The theological statement is not continued beyond the point at which it serves the immediate practical purpose.

[12] You have Christ's example to inspire and guide you. So then, my beloved ones, just as on all occasions hitherto you have showed ready obedience to God, do so now in this way. Not only when you can rely upon me during my presence with you ; on the contrary, far more during my absence from you ;—relying upon yourselves, with godly fear and trembling anxiety to be obedient, work out your salvation. [13] In this you have far better help than mine. For it is God who works in you, in fulfilment of His benevolent purpose (therefore you need not fear and must not glory) ; and He supplies you with both the will and the power to be obedient. [14] In all that you have to do be not like the Israelites with their murmurings and questionings, [15] that you may become blameless in the sight of men and innocent in the sight of God. Yes, become children of God, not rebels, children without blemish, in the midst of a crooked and perverse generation,— amongst whom you appear as luminaries in the world,—[16] holding out to others the Gospel in all its life-giving power. With this blessed result, that on the Day of Christ's Return to test all works I may be able to boast that, as regards yourselves, I did not run my race in vain, nor yet struggle and toil in vain. [17] Do not think that I grudge the toil. I would give far more than that. Even if I am poured out on the sacrifice and service of your faith, when this is offered to God, I rejoice and congratulate all of you ; [18] and in the same manner I invite you to rejoice and to congratulate me.

12. So then] *Itaque* Vulg. here and iv. 1. The ὥστε evidently refers to the description of Christ as a model ; see on iv. 1 and on 1 Thess. iv. 18.

my beloved ones] Cf. iv. 1 ; 1 Cor. x. 14.

have showed] This is one of many cases in which it is the Greek idiom to use the aorist, but the English idiom to use the perfect. Cf. ἔμαθον, iv. 11.

obedience to God] As Christ did (v. 8). Beet follows Meyer in taking obedience to be to the "apostolic authority of Paul." But v. 13 points to God, and Θεός is emphatic by position. See Hort on 1 Pet. i. 14. 'To obey,' ὑπακούειν, is 'to listen submissively.'

In what follows two constructions are intermingled ; but it is not difficult to disentangle them.

Not only] This belongs to ' work out,' not to ' showed ready obedience.'

during my presence] See on i. 26.

far more] πολλῷ μᾶλλον, as in i. 23.

relying upon yourselves] The reflexive pronoun ἑαυτῶν is very emphatic, and something to mark this is needed early in the sentence. See Pfleiderer, *Paulinism*, I. p. 224.

fear and trembling anxiety] The combination φόβος καὶ τρόμος is frequent in LXX, and there the usual meaning is fear of severe treatment ; Gen. ix. 2 ; Exod. xv. 16 ; Deut. ii. 25, xi. 25 ; etc. But that is not how St. Paul uses the expression. He is the only N.T. writer who has the phrase, and he appears to mean by it *a nervous anxiety to do one's duty*; 1 Cor. ii. 3 ; 2 Cor. vii. 15 ; Eph. vi. 5, where this fear is opposed to eye-service.* Fear of failure may be included, and some Fathers make this the whole idea.

work out] The preposition in κατεργάζεσθε is intensive, strengthening the simple verb, ' carry to the end,' *usque ad metam* (Bengel). Vulg. has *operari* here and generally ; also *facere, perficere, efficere*, and *consummare*. The compound occurs twenty times in Paul and only thrice in the rest of N.T. The κατά sometimes gives a bad sense ; Rom. i. 27, ii. 9 ; 1 Cor. v. 3. Cf. *per* in *perficere* and *perpetrare*.

your own salvation] The reciprocal force of ἑαυτῶν (Eph. iv. 32 ; Col. iii. 13, 16), ' one another's salvation,' is certainly not the meaning here.

13. For it is God] ' God ' is emphatic ; and ' for ' (γάρ) explains how they can work out their own salvation without either despondency or presumption. They must anxiously, but hopefully, seek to secure their own eternal welfare, for God is sure to help, because it is His desire and delight to do so. See Hort on 1 Pet. i. 9.†

---

* *Die ganze christliche Gewissenhaftigkeit darin liegt* (De Wette).

† *Non, il ne le peut de lui-même et par lui-même : mais il n'oublie point d'ailleurs ce que lui apprend le Docteur des nations, qu'il peut tout en celui qui le fortifie. De sorte qu'il ne balance pas un moment à se mettre en œuvre et à commencer. Ce n'est point par une témérité présomptueuse, puisque son espérance est fondée sur ce grand principe*

works in you] Another Pauline expression; ἐνεργεῖν
with a personal subject, ἐνεργεῖσθαι with an impersonal;
seventeen times in Paul and only thrice elsewhere in N.T.
'In you,' not 'among you.' St. Paul is not troubled
with the relation of these facts to the question of man's
free will.

in fulfilment of] 'For '(R.V.) is better than 'of' (A.V.). We
have ὑπέρ, 'in order to accomplish,' not διά. Blass, § 42, 5.
This clause is not to be taken with what follows, as Conybeare
and Howson take it.

both the will] The Divine help can be counted on from
the very start; Aug. *De Grat. et Lib. Arb.* xvii.; 10th
Article of Religion. We must co-operate. It rests with us
to decide whether we yield to good or to evil influences.

14. In all] 'All' is emphatic; all the details of daily
life; 1 Cor. x. 31; cf. Col. iii. 17.

like the Israelites] The context seems to show that the
Apostle has their unrest and rebellious utterances against
Moses in his mind; Exod. xvi. 7; Num. xvi. 11; Cf. 1 Cor.
x. 10.

questionings] Referring perhaps rather to spoken disputings than to mental reasonings; Rom. i. 21, xvi. 1; 1 Cor.
iii. 20. Vulg. has *haesitationes*, Rhem. 'staggerings.' In
papyri διαλογισμοί seems always to mean uttered discus-
sions; there are no examples of 'thoughts,' 'cogitations.'
M. and M., p. 151. It was evidently open disagreements
that troubled the Philippian Church. In Biblical Greek
the word has commonly, but not invariably, a bad sense.
Hatch, *Bibl. Grk.* p. 8.

15. may become] 'May be' (A.V.) follows the inferior
reading ἦτε : γένησθε is probably right, and ἦτε may come
from i. 10.

innocent] Lit. 'unmixed,' 'unadulterated,' ἀκέραιοι,
as in Rom. xvi. 19; Mt. x. 16. Trench, *Syn.* § lvi. Cf.
εἰλικρινεῖς, i. 10.

children of God] Not '*the sons* of God' (A.V.). This

de Saint Paul (Bourdaloue). Bossuet has a similar passage, *Médita-
tions, Sermon sur la Montagne,* xxxii.

quotation from the Song of Moses, Deut. xxxii. 5, is further evidence that the conduct of the rebellious Israelites in the wilderness is the danger which the Philippians must avoid.

without blemish] Rather than ' without *rebuke* ' (A.V.). This is the third negative adjective ; free from blame, from adulteration, from blemish. They are to be fit to be presented to God. Hort on 1 Pet. 1. 19 ; Westcott on Eph. i. 4 ; Trench, § ciii.

perverse] Stronger than ' crooked ' ; Acts ii. 40, xx. 30 ; Mt. xvii. 17 ; Lk. ix. 41. ' Generation,' not ' nation ' (A.V.).

you appear] Or ' are seen,' not ' ye shine ' (A.V. following Vulg. *lucetis*). We have φαίνεσθε, not φαίνετε, and the verb is probably indicative, not imperative.

luminaries] Rather than ' lights ' ; φωστῆρες, not φῶτα. In LXX the word is commonly used of sun, moon, and stars ; Gen. i. 14, 16 ; Wisd. xiii. 2 ; Ecclus. xliii. 7. It " is suggestive of a light shining in darkness " (Abbott, *The Fourfold Gospel*, V. p. 254). Beza is misleading with *faces*. See Swete on Rev. xxi. 11, the only other N.T. passage in which the word occurs ; Trench, § xlvi.

16. **holding out to others**] The meaning of ἐπέχοντες is uncertain. From ' applying,' ' directing,' it comes to mean ' holding forth,' ' offering,' *e.g.* food or drink. This makes good sense here. ' Instead of disputing among yourselves, dispense your spiritual blessings to others.' *Praetendentes* Beza, *sustinentes* Calvin. Some render ἐπέχοντες ' holding fast,' *continentes* Vulg. ; and this also makes good sense. ' Instead of disputing about unimportant matters, keep firm hold on that which is essential.' ' Because ye possess ' is inadequate.*

the Gospel etc.] ' A word of life ' means a communication which has life as its subject and effect ; and ' life ' has here

---

* Field (*Otium Norvic.* III. p. 118) rejects both these renderings, and gives, as a literal translation, " holding the analogy of life," *i.e.*, " being (to the world) in the stead of life." He rightly rejects the suggestion that φωστῆρες points to such lights as the Pharos at Alexandria.

its highest and most comprehensive sense. Λόγον has no article. Cf. Jn. vi. 63, 68.

Day of Christ's Return] See on i. 6.   The εἰς means not ' until,' but ' *against* the Day.' The boasting is reserved for that Day.

able to boast] Cf. i. 26 ; 1 Thess. ii. 19 ; 2 Cor. i. 14.   A.V. again has ' rejoice.'

as regards yourselves] This limitation is implied.   The results of his work among other converts are not under consideration.

I did not run] We have the same expression Gal. ii. 2. The metaphor implies great effort ; 1 Cor. ix. 25 ; Gal. v. 7. The aorist looks back from the point of view of the Day.

in vain] Lit ' unto emptiness,' εἰς κένον, being empty-handed after all ; 1 Thess. iii. 5 ; 2 Cor. vi. 1.   The repetition gives emphasis.

struggle and toil] It is possible that ἐκοπίασα continues the metaphor of contests in the arena ; cf. Is. xl. 31.   More probably the thought is of *missionary* (Cor. 1 xv. 10, xvi. 16) and of *manual* labour, of which he had had much experience ; see on 1 Thess ii. 9 ; 2 Thess. iii. 8 ; 2 Cor. xi. 27.

17. But . . . even if] Something has to be understood between ἀλλά and εἰ καί.   ' *But* why talk of labours ? I am ready *even if* the worst comes,' viz. the being condemned to death.   Εἰ καί introduces a condition which is stated problematically, but is conceded as a fact, ' even though '; 2 Cor. iv. 3, 16, v. 16, vii. 8, xiii. 11 ; Col. ii. 5.   The καί emphasizes σπένδομαι, which is admitted for the sake of argument.   Winer, pp. 554 f.

am poured out] Not ' I am being poured out.'   The present tense does not mean that the sacrifice is already begun ; and there is therefore no inconsistency between this statement and the expectation of release in i. 25, 26, ii. 24.   In 2 Tim. iv. 6, when the death was very near, ἤδη depicts the pouring as beginning, ἤδη σπένδομαι.   The present after εἰ often merely states the supposition graphic-ally.   The allusion is probably to heathen sacrifices, in which the libation was a more distinct feature than in Jewish sacrifices. A prisoner in Rome would often see or hear of heathen libations. Moreover, nearly all the Philippian Christians were converts from heathenism. It is to heathen rites that he refers 2 Cor. ii. 14.

The sacrifice is the Philippians' faith. The Apostle's life-blood is the libation poured over it. Who offers the sacrifice ? Surely the Philippian Church ; not the Apostle whose life-blood enriches the sacrifice.

sacrifice and service] It is not easy to find a satisfactory rendering for λειτουργία here. In LXX it and its cognate forms occur about 140 times, and they commonly imply *sacerdotal* ministration. Here it may be added to θυσία to suggest that the Philippians in offering their faith perform a priestly act. They share in the universal priesthood of the Christian Church. Vulg. has the vague *obsequium*. See on 2 Cor. ix. 12.

congratulate] It is difficult to decide between ' congratulate ' and ' rejoice along with ' for συγχαίρω, but the latter makes rather poorer sense when *v.* 18 is taken into account. ' Have the same joy, and the same rejoicing with me ' is tautological. ' I rejoice with all of you ' implies that the Philippians are already rejoicing ; whereas in *v.* 18 they are exhorted to rejoice. Vulg. has *congratulor* here ; *congaudeo* 1 Cor. xii. 26, xiii. 6. English Versions have ' rejoice ' or ' be glad.' The question is unimportant. Note the ' all.' As in i. 3–8, he refuses to recognize their differences ; all without exceptions are included.

18. in the same measure] He and they are to have the same joy and the same subject of congratulation. He cannot bear to be alone in rejoicing, and they ought to be able to rejoice with him in the prospect of his possible martyrdom. ' The same ' is placed first with emphasis. Cf. Mt. xxvii. 44.

This charge concludes the exhortations. He once more changes from the Philippians to himself and speaks of personal matters. Having told of his past and present, he now speaks of his future.

ii. 19–30. EXPLANATORY AND PERSONAL

The Apostle's plans have reference to compensating the Philippians for his enforced absence from them. He means to send them the best substitute, Timothy, whom they know so well and who will do his utmost to serve them (19–24). But as Timothy cannot come at once, he is sending back to them their delegate Epaphroditus, about whom they have been anxious, and who has worked himself almost to death in order to prove Philippian devotion to the Apostle (25–30).

ii. 19–24. TIMOTHY TO BE SENT VERY SOON.

¹⁹ But I trust in the Lord Jesus to send Timotheus shortly unto you, that I also may be of good comfort, when I know your state. ²⁰ For I have no man likeminded, who will naturally care for your state. ²¹ For all seek their own, not the things which are Jesus Christ's. ²² But ye know the proof of him, That as a son with the father he hath served with me in the Gospel. ²³ Him therefore I hope to send presently, so soon as I shall see how it will go with me. ²⁴ But I trust in the Lord that I also myself shall come shortly.

It is remarkable that St. Paul uses more decided language about eventually coming himself than about his sending Timothy soon. He *hopes* (*vv.* 19, 23) to do the latter ; he is *confident* (*v.* 24) about doing the former.

¹⁹ But, although I cannot at present come myself, I quite hope in the Lord Jesus to send you Timothy very soon, in order that I as well as you may be cheered in mind thereby, for from him I shall get to know about your spiritual welfare. ²⁰ I select him, for I have no one with me here who is at all his equal in mind, I mean none who will be likely to be so genuinely anxious about your spiritual welfare. ²¹ For, of the others, one and all pursue their own interests, and care nothing about those of Jesus Christ. ²² But by the credentials of long experience you know how, as a son to a father, he has slaved with me for the promotion of the Gospel. ²³ Him, therefore, I quite hope to send forthwith, as soon as ever I see how things will go with myself. ²⁴ But as regards that, I am confident in the Lord that I myself also shall come to you very soon.

19. But I quite hope] This looks back to *v.* 12, in which he exhorted them to continue to be obedient during his absence. He is obliged at present to remain absent, *but* he quite hopes to send a very good substitute soon. It also looks back to *v.* 17 ; he might ' be poured out,' and in that case could not return to them. A.V. has ' I trust ' for both ἐλπίζω and πέποιθα, thus obliterating an interesting change in the Apostle's attitude of mind. Both the hope and the confidence are ' in the Lord.' Chrysostom says, " See how he makes all depend upon God "; he should have said "upon Christ." Cf. i. 13, Rom. xiv. 14, xvi. 2–22 ; I Cor. iv. 17, vii. 22, 39, etc. All that he thinks and does is ' in Christ,' i. 21.

send you Timothy] As in the very similar passage I Cor. iv. 17, we have ὑμῖν, ' for your comfort.' A.V. has ' unto you,' which would be πρὸς ὑμᾶς, as in *v.* 25. Cf. I Thess. iii. 6 ; 2 Thess. i. 3.

cheered in mind] Εὐψυχεῖν occurs here only in Biblical Greek, and seems not to be found in classical Greek.* The cognate woids are not rare either in classical Greek or in LXX. This shows that he expects to live to receive Timothy's report.

20. with me here] This limitation is implied ; he says ' I have,' not ' I know.'

his equal in mind] Ἰσόψυχος is another very rare word. ' So dear unto me ' (A.V. margin) is not the meaning ; that would be ἴσος τῆς ψυχῆς μου, Deut. xiii. 6. Nor is ' heart and soul with me ' (Way) right ; that would be σύμψυχος. *Neminem pari animo praeditum* (Beza), or *Neminem aeque animatum ad res vestras curandas* (Calvin), is better.

who will be likely] Here, as often in N.T., ὅστις has its full meaning, ' who is of such a quality as.' A. T. Robertson, *Gr.* pp. 726 f. Cf. i. 28 ; 2 Thess. i. 9 ; etc.

genuinely] Both adverb (γνησίως) and adjective are exclusively Pauline in N.T., meaning ' legitimately born,'

---

* Εὐψυχεῖν occurs Joseph. *Ant.* XI. vi. 9 of Ahasuerus encouraging Esther, and the imperative εὐψύχει, ' Be of good cheer,' is found in inscriptions. M. and M., *Vocabulary*, p. 268.

F

and so ' genuine,' ' sincere.'   Cf. iv. 3 ; Tim. i. 2 of Timothy himself.   See M. and M., p. 129.

anxious] Cf. 2 Cor. xi. 28 ; 1 Cor. xii. 25 ; 2 Macc. xiv. 8. There is a right and a wrong anxiety, just as a right and a wrong attention to one's own interests (*v.* 4).   See on iv. 6 and cf. Mt. vi. 25, 34 ; Lk. xii. 22.

21. **of the others**] The same limitation as before ; he is speaking of those who are in Rome.

one and all] Πάντες has the article, making ' all ' rigorous ; there are no exceptions.   This looks like emotional hyperbole ; but he perhaps means only " all who were available for missionary purposes " (Ellicott) ; they had all begged to be excused from going to Philippi.   Evidently Luke and Aristarchus are no longer with him.   The letter was written late in the Roman imprisonment.   Cf. 2 Tim. iv. 10.

pursue their own interests] ' Seek their own advantages ' ; ii. 4 ; 1 Cor. x. 24, xiii. 5.   Note the change from τὰ περὶ ὑμῶν to τὰ ἑαυτῶν.   *O quam multi sua causa pii sunt!* (Bengel).

22. **But by the credentials, etc.**] The ' But ' (δέ) might be understood in two ways.   Either, ' *But* I need not commend him to you '; ye are alive to his tried worth '; Abbott, *Johannine Grammar*, p. 197.   Or, ' *But* he is very different from all the rest.'

credentials] The A.V. has four renderings of δοκιμή, ' proof,' ' trial,' ' experiment,' and ' experience.'   Vulg. has *probatio* and *experimentum*.   That the Philippians' knowledge of Timothy was the result of experience is implied in γινώσκετε. In commending Timothy he is merely reproducing their own proved estimate of him.   Strangely enough, Vulg., Pelagius, Wiclif, and Calvin take γινώσκετε as an imperative ; as if Timothy was a stranger to the Philippians !

he has slaved with me] The ' with ' (σύν) must not be anticipated and placed before ' a father,' as in A.V.   When St. Paul dictated ὡς πατρὶ τεκνόν, he had some other construction vaguely in his mind.   His main thought was that Timothy had been like a son to him ; 2 Tim. i. 2.   He then thinks that he will commend Timothy as an equal and a colleague. To supply 'with' before 'a father' spoils this sudden and pleasing change of view. *Concinne loquitur, partim ut de filio, partim ut de collega* (Bengel). A.V. has 'with *the* father.'

slaved with me] Both being δοῦλοι Χριστοῦ Ἰησοῦ, i. 1. All this shows that Timothy had no part in the composition of the letter.

for the promotion of] Not 'in ' (A.V.) ; εἰς as in i. 5, not ἐν.

23. **Him, therefore**] The pronoun is emphatic, and anticipates 'I also myself' in *v*. 24. The μὲν . . . δέ might be rendered 'On the one hand I hope to send him ; on the other I am confident of coming myself.' A.V. has 'I hope' for ἐλπίζω here, in *v*. 19 'I trust.'

forthwith] 'Presently' is now not strong enough for ἐξαυτῆς. In 1611 '*presently*' had its proper meaning of 'immediately.' Aldis Wright, *Bible Word Book*, p. 473, and T. L. O. Davies, *Bible English*, p. 109, give illustrations.

as soon as ever I see] The verb ἀφίδω or ἀπίδω is used of seeing from a distance, seeing the issue of events ; also of concentrating one's attention on one object. The former better fits the context here. Cf. Jonah iv. 5. The aspirated form ἀφίδω is frequent in papyri.

how things will go] Τὰ περὶ ἐμέ : not quite the same as τὰ κατ' ἐμέ, i. 12. Could he have said this at Caesarea ? It almost necessarily implies Rome.

24. **I am confident**] Cf. i. 6, 25. For 'in the Lord' and 'very soon' cf. *v*. 19. The verse is in emphatic contrast to 'I hope' *vv*. 19, 23. This visit he paid between his first and second imprisonment at Rome, 1 Tim. i. 3.

very soon] This ταχέως is against his having thoughts of first going to Spain. But it must be interpreted in harmony with what has just been stated. Timothy is to be, not a mere messenger, but a substitute for the Apostle during some time. Cf. 1 Cor. iv. 17–19.

ii. 25–30. EPAPHRODITUS TO BE SENT AT ONCE].

²⁵ Yet I supposed it necessary to send to you Epaphroditus, my brother and companion in labour, and fellow soldier, but your

messenger, and he that ministered to my wants. ²⁶ For he longed after you all, and was full of heaviness, because that ye had heard that he had been sick. ²⁷ For indeed he was sick nigh unto death, but God had mercy on him : and not on him only, but on me also, lest I should have sorrow upon sorrow. ²⁸ I sent him therefore the more carefully, that, when ye see him again, ye may rejoice, and that I may be the less sorrowful. ²⁹ Receive him therefore in the Lord with all gladness, and hold such in reputation : ³⁰ Because for the work of Christ he was nigh unto death, not regarding his life, to supply your lack of service to me.

Epaphras perhaps might be an abbreviation of Epaphroditus ; but that is no reason for identifying the persons who respectively bear the names in N.T.   Epaphras (Col. i. 7, iv. 12 ; Philem. 23) was an Oriental, a Colossian.   Epaphroditus was a European, a Philippian ; and we know no more of him than what is told us here.

²⁵ But, as neither of us can come immediately, I account it necessary to send to you Epaphroditus, who is one with me in faith and shares my labours and my conflicts, but whom you sent to me to serve me in my need.   ²⁶ I am sending him with all the more satisfaction, because he has been yearning to see all of you again, and was deeply distressed because you heard that he had been ill. ²⁷ For indeed he was very ill, and very nearly died. But God in His mercy spared him,—a mercy not to him only, but also to me, to save me from having an additional burden of sorrow. ²⁸ For this reason I am sending him to you the more eagerly, in order that by the sight of him in good health you may regain your joy, and that I, through sympathy with your and his delight, may have my sorrow lessened. ²⁹ Give him therefore a hearty welcome in the Lord with every form of joy, and hold men like him in great esteem ; ³⁰ because it was through his devotion to the work of the Gospel that he very nearly died, hazarding his life in order that by his affectionate zeal he might fulfil that part of your service towards me which you were unable to render in person.

25. I account it necessary] Here, as in *v.* 28, we have an epistolary aorist, which must be rendered by the present tense in English.   Burton, § 44 ; Winer, p. 347.   Cf. 2 Cor. viii. 17, 18, 22, ix. 3.

Epaphroditus] The name means ' favoured by Aphrodite,' ' comely.'   There was an incredible tradition that he was

Nero's secretary.* Theodoret hesitatingly makes him an
ἐπίσκοπος at Philippi.

one with me in faith] 'The brother' means 'who is a
Christian'; i. 14; 1 Cor. v. 11; Gal. i. 2.

shares my labours] Or 'my fellow-worker'; cf. iv. 3;
Rom. xvi. 3, 9, 21; Philem. i. 24; etc.

shares my conflicts] As a fellow-soldier must do; συνστρα-
τώτης here and Philem. 2. The three terms are under one
article, and perhaps are meant to form a climax; 'one
with me in faith, in work, in warfare.' The Apostle perhaps
feared that the Philippians might be dissatisfied with the
way in which Epaphroditus had acted as their representative
in Rome. He tells them how devoted he had been, and
charges them to give him a hearty welcome.

you sent to me to serve me in my need] Lit. 'your apostle
and minister of my need.' There is strong emphasis on
ὑμῶν, contrasting what Epaphroditus was to the Philippians
with what he was to St. Paul. A.V. spoils this by limiting
ὑμῶν to ἀπόστολον. Ἀπόστολον καὶ λειτουργόν balance
συνεργὸν καὶ στρατιώτην. 'Apostle' does not mean that
Epaphroditus held any office in the Church,† but that he was
the *emissary* selected by the Philippians to bring their
offerings to the imprisoned Apostle. He was their delegate
(*legatus*, Beza, Bengel), to minister to his wants; cf. iv. 16
and 2 Cor. viii. 3. For λειτουργ. see on *v.* 17; it was a
holy service.

26. yearning to see] 'To see' is of somewhat doubtful
authority; the true reading may be 'yearning for all of you,'
as in i. 8. The periphrastic imperfect, ἐπιποθῶν ἦν, indicates the persistent continuance of homesickness.

* There was a freedman of Octavianus, and another of Nero,
of this name. The latter helped Nero to kill himself and was put
to death by Domitian. Neither of these can have been the Philippian
who ministered to St. Paul. See Dion. Cass. ii. 11, 13; Tac. *Ann.*
xv. 55; Suet. *Nero*, xlix.; Domit. xiv. C. H. Hoole, *The Classical
Element in the N.T.* p. 34.

† Epaphroditus is one of many whom later tradition has placed
among the Seventy. Any N.T. name, about which the contrary
was not known, might be put on that list.

deeply distressed] Or, ' sore troubled ' ; the word that is
used of the Agony, Mk. xiv. 33 ; Mt. xxvi. 37.   If ἀδημονεῖν
(from a and δῆμος through ἀδήμων) can mean ' be away
from one's people,' ' away from home,' the word is very
appropriate to a homesick person.

had been ill] In such cases the English pluperfect best
represents the Greek aorist, as in A.V.

27. **For indeed**] Καὶ γάρ introduces what amounts to
an additional reason ; ' he was not only ill, he was at death's
door.' Παραπλήσιον occurs here only in Biblical Greek.

additional burden] ' His death, on the top of my imprisonment.'   Not, ' on the top of his illness ' (Chrys.).   All this
(the Philippians hear of St. Paul's need ; they collect money
and send Epaphroditus ; he overworks himself in Rome
and falls ill ; the Philippians hear of this ; he hears that they
are anxious about him ; he recovers) implies a very considerable amount of time.   This letter cannot have been
written early in the Apostle's imprisonment.

There is no hint that the Apostle used his miraculous
powers of healing to cure his friend.   Such powers were not
given him to further his own interests.   What is certain is,
that, with characteristic unselfishness, he was willing to
part with such consoling and useful friends as Timothy and
Epaphroditus, in order to help his beloved Philippians.

28. **am sending**] With this letter ; epistolary aorist, as
in v. 25 ; cf. Eph. vi. 22 ; Col. iv. 8 ; Philem. 11.

the more eagerly] *Festinantius*, Vulg.   The Apostle's sympathy is conspicuous ; with the sickness and homesickness
of Epaphroditus, with the Philippians' anxiety about him,
and with their joy at seeing him again well.   Cf. 2 Cor. xi.
29.

regain your joy] The πάλιν is amphibolous, but it goes
better with χαρῆτε than with ἰδόντες.   The Vulg. is equally
uncertain, *ut viso eo iterum gaudeatis* ; but there also ' again '
goes better with what follows.   Beza has *eo rursus viso
gaudeatis* ; so also A.V. and R.V.

my sorrow lessened] One is tempted to say ' one sorrow
the less ' ; but that would be too definite.   The additional

sorrow in *v.* 27 was removed when Epaphroditus recovered. The original sorrow, which still remains his portion, will be lessened by sympathy with the Philippians' joy at having Epaphroditus home again and in good health.

29. **Give him therefore**] Προσδέχεσθε might mean ' expect him '; Mk. xv. 43 ; Lk. ii. 25 ; Tit. ii. 13. But that cannot be the meaning here, for Epaphroditus was the bearer of the letter. Cf. Rom. xvi. 2.

in the Lord] A truly Christian welcome ; i. 13, ii. 19, 24.

every form of joy] Cf. i. 20. ' Gladness ' (A.V.) obscures the reiteration in the letter of χαρά (i. 4, 25, ii. 2, iv. 1) and χαίρειν (i. 18, ii. 17, 18, 28, iii. 1, iv. 1, 4, 10). With πάσης χαρᾶς cf. Rom. xv. 13 ; Jas. i. 2.

hold] Both verbs are present imperative ; ' give an enduring welcome ; hold continually in honour.'

in great esteem] The compound ἔντιμος (Lk. vii. 2, xiv. 8) is specially used of the personal preciousness (1 Sam. xxvi. 21 ; Is. xliii. 4) of those who are held in honour, as in classical Greek. Hort on 1 Pet. ii. 4.

30. **the work**] The best MSS. have τὸ ἔργον without addition ; cf. ' the Name,' *v.* 9, ' the Way,' Acts ix. 2, xix. 9, 23, xxiv. 22 ; ' the Work,' Acts xv. 38, in a speech of St. Paul. Other MSS. add κυρίου or τοῦ κυρίου (R.V. margin), or Χριστοῦ (A.V., R.V.).

hazarding his life] Παραβολευσάμενος, ' having played the gambler ' (παράβολος = ' venturesome '). Copyists not being familiar with this verb substituted παραβουλευσάμενος, and hence ' not regarding his life ' (A.V.). There is nothing to suggest that he was out of health when he started from Philippi, or was overcome by the fatigue of the journey. His health broke down in Rome, in the effort to make up for the absence of other Philippians. *Tradens animam suam* (Vulg.) is vague. Cf. *Regulum et Scauros animaeque magnae Prodigum Paullum,* Hor. *Od.* I. xii. 37. The *Parabolani* at Alexandria were a large guild who *risked* their lives in visiting the sick and burying the dead during the plague. Deissmann, *Light,* p. 84 ; Suicer, II. 565.

might fulfil] The delicate conciseness of the Greek cannot

be reproduced in English. Both A.V., 'to supply your
lack of service,' and R.V., 'to supply that which was lacking
in your service,' suggest that the Philippians had been re-
miss in ministering to the Apostle's needs ; whereas they had
been liberal. To hint that his converts had been niggardly
in their gifts would be very unlike the Apostle's tactfulness
and delicacy. But the donors had had to send their contributions ; they could not come and minister to him in person :
and Epaphroditus had nearly killed himself in the struggle
fully to make up for their absence. Ἀναπληροῦν is 'to fill
up that which is partly empty,' to complete what is incom-
plete. See Robertson and Plummer on 1 Cor. xvi. 17,
where the same phrase occurs. As in v. 17, Vulg. has
obsequium for λειτουργία. Self-sacrificing service is implied.

Weinel says of this passage (25–30), " The man who can
write such words from his heart wins the affections of his
fellows. It is scarcely possible to write with greater consideration or tenderness. There are no parallels in all
epistolary literature to the passages in which Paul speaks
of his friends and fellow-labourers to his converts " (*St. Paul,
the Man and his Work*, p. 376).

iii. 1. RENEWED EXHORTATION TO REJOICE.

[1] Finally, my brethren, rejoice in the Lord. To write the same
things to you, to me indeed is not grievous ; but for you it is safe.

Either in the middle of this verse, or at the end of it,
there is a sudden break. The exact position of the break
depends upon the interpretation of the second half of the
verse. If it refers to what is coming, the break is in the
middle of the verse. If it refers to what has already been
said, the break is at the end.

[1] For the rest, my Brethren, I charge you to rejoice as all Christians
should. Forgive me if I repeat myself. To be writing the same
things to you is not at all irksome to me, and it may save you from
mistake.

1. **For the rest**] ' As to what remains to be said.' This
division of the letter, like 2 Thess. iii. 1, opens with τὸ λοιπόν,

which seems to imply that the writer is thinking of bringing his letter to a conclusion. Λοιπόν (1 Thess. iv. 1 ; 1 Cor. 1. 16 ; 2 Cor. xiii. 11) is perhaps more colloquial. A.V. and R.V. have ' Finally ' for both, and Vulg. nearly always has *de cetero*, which is better.   In 1 Cor. i. 16 the expression is too remote from the conclusion for ' Finally,' and there A.V. and R.V. have ' besides.'   Here the Apostle at once digresses, and τὸ λοιπόν is repeated iv. 8.

my Brethren] St. Paul does not often add μου to ἀδελφοί. In Rom., 1 Cor., and Phil. twice each.   St. James has it very often.

rejoice] Χαίρετε may mean either ' rejoice ' or ' farewell,' and some think that here both meanings are intended.   Cf. ii. 18, iv. 4.   As so often (see on i. 14, ii. 10, 24 ; 2 Cor. xiii. 11) everything is ' in the Lord,' the Christian's natural environment ;   one in which, as Chrysostom remarks, even afflictions have joy.   He connects this clause closely with what precedes ; ' You have no reason to be out of heart ; you have Epaphroditus ; you shall have Timothy ; I am coming also.   What do you need more ?   Rejoice.' The connexion is doubtful.

the same things] These are the crucial words ; what is meant by τὰ αὐτά ?   Various answers are possible.   The same (1) as I have said by word of mouth ; (2) as I have told Epaphroditus to say to you ; (3) as I have said in a former letter ; (4) as I say in this letter.   Neither (1) nor (2) seems to be very probable.   Beet, Vincent and Zahn adopt (3) ;   but, as Theodore, Theodoret, and Pelagius remark, we do not even know (οὐδεμόθεν ἐμάθομεν) that there had been an earlier letter, although it is quite possible that there had been one or more.   Assuming (4) to be right, what subjects are repeated in this letter ?   There are two dominant notes, the duty of *rejoicing* and the duty of *unity*.   As the former has just been enjoined (χαίρετε), this may be the topic for the repetition of which the Apostle apologizes.   If it be asked, what peril was there in not rejoicing, we may reply that gloom is a dangerous temper, and that the Philippians had still to learn the importance

of Christian joy.   If we look at what *follows* (iii. 2–iv. 1) they
are warned against two errors, the acceptance of either of
which would be fatal to their *unity* ; and this therefore
may be the meaning of ' the same things,' and hence the
curious digression.*   Certainty is not attainable.

Meyer, Lightfoot, Beet, and M. Jones, with Conybeare
and Howson, place the break in the middle of the verse ;
W.H., Moffatt, and Lueken place it at the end of it.   R.V.
has no break.   Ellicott thinks that " this exhortation not
unnaturally follows."   Vaughan sees " entire coherence and
beautiful harmony."

irksome] ' Causing delay ' is a common meaning of
ὀκνηρός, and hence ' sluggish,' ' reluctant '; Rom. xii. 11 ;
Mt. xxv. 26 ; and often in Proverbs.   Here it means ' causing reluctance.'   Even if it were irksome to him, the safety
of so many would outweigh this.†

save you from mistake] Repetition prevents misunder-
standing.   Vulg. has the inexact *necessarium*, which may
be an echo of i. 24.

iii. 2–iv. 9.   WARNINGS AND EXHORTATIONS

There are two Warnings, one against Judaism (iii. 2–11),
and one against Antinomianism (iii. 12–21).   The Exhortations are to Unity (iv. 2, 3), to Joy (iv. 4–7), and to the
Practice of what is Noblest and Best (iv. 8, 9).

iii. 2–11.   WARNING AGAINST JUDAISM.

² Beware of dogs, beware of evil workers : beware of the Conci-
sion.   ³ For we are the circumcision, which worship God in the spirit,

---

* On the whole this seems to be the best explanation.   The
Judaizers were a ceaseless horror.   They were an actual or a possible
trouble wherever the Apostle worked.   In his previous visits he
may often have warned the Philippians against them.

† The words are a rough iambic trimeter, such as is common in
Greek Comedy, and may possibly be a quotation.   For other instances of possible quotations cf. 1 Cor. xv. 33 ; Tit. i. 12.   The
hexameter in Jas. i. 17 is probably accidental.

and rejoice in Christ Jesus, and have no confidence in the flesh.
⁴ Though I might also have confidence in the flesh. If any other
man thinketh that he hath whereof he might trust in the flesh, I
more : ⁵ Circumcised the eighth day, of the stock of Israel, of the
tribe of Benjamin, an Hebrew of the Hebrews ; as touching the law,
a Pharisee : ⁶ Concerning zeal, persecuting the Church ; touching
the righteousness which is in the law, blameless. ⁷ But what things
were gain to me, those I counted loss for Christ. ⁸ Yea doubtless,
and I count all things but loss, for the excellency of the knowledge of
Christ Jesus my Lord : for whom I have suffered the loss of all
things, and do count them but dung, that I may win Christ, ⁹ And
be found in him, not having my own righteousness, which is of the
law, but that which is through the faith of Christ, the righteousness
which is of God by faith : ¹⁰ That I may know him, and the power of
his resurrection, and the fellowship of his sufferings, being made
conformable unto his death, ¹¹ If by any means I might attain unto
the resurrection of the dead.

The abrupt change of tone is no sufficient reason for
thinking that we have here a portion of a different letter.
Very possibly the Apostle was interrupted at this point by
" some new exasperating experience " (Jülicher), and when
he resumed, a different subject was in his mind. " Many
passages of his Epistles are like the sudden eruption of a
volcano " (Von Soden, *Early Christian Literature*, p. 23).
See also Hort, *Judaistic Christianity*, p. 114, and cf. 2 Cor.
xi. 13-15 ; 1 Thess. iii. 14-16.

² Be on your guard about the unclean dogs, on your guard about
the wicked workers, on your guard about the self-mutilation. ³ I
call it mutilation, for we Christians are the true circumcision ; we
who by the Spirit of God, and not with the traditions of men, offer
the true worship ; we who have our boast in Christ Jesus, and put
no confidence in the external privileges of race and habitation.
⁴ I say this, not as depreciating what I do not possess. I say it,
although I myself can have confidence even in these privileges,
if I care to do so. If any other man thinks that he can place confidence in Jewish privileges, I can do so more securely. ⁵ I was circumcised the eighth day after birth ; I am descended from the
original stock of Israel, not grafted into it ; I know to which tribe I
belong, the renowned tribe of Benjamin : I am the Hebrew son of
Hebrew parents. To these inherited distinctions I added others by my
own choice. As regards the law, I joined the strict sect of Pharisees ;
⁶ as regards zeal for the national faith, I persecuted the Christian

Church ; as regards such righteousness as consists in mere observance
of the law, I showed myself blameless. ⁷ But such things as used to
be in my eyes items of gain, these, in order to win Christ, I have set
down as just so much loss.   ⁸ Nay, moreover, I even continue to set
down, not merely these things, but all things, as so much loss, when
compared with the supreme value of knowing Christ Jesus my Lord.
To win Him I suffered the loss of everything, one and all, and I now
set them down as utter refuse, in order that I may gain Christ,⁹ and be
found at the great Day to be a member of His body, not having any
righteousness of my own such as comes from the law, but such as
comes through faith in Christ, the righteousness which comes from
God on condition of this faith, ¹⁰ that I may know and appropriate
Christ. This implies knowing the power of His resurrection and
having fellowship in His sufferings, with my nature conformed to
His death, ¹¹ if so be that I may attain, as He did, to the rising again,
the rising again from the dead.

2. **Be on your guard**] Cf. our colloquial, ' Just look at,'
' keep your eye on.' The βλέπετε occurs thrice. It
precedes each of the opprobrious designations of these
disturbers of the Church's peace ; and each of the designations has the article, showing that some notorious mischief-
makers are here condemned. But the three designations
are of one and the same class, whether Jews or (more probably) Judaizing Christians. There were such people
among professing Christians ; but the tone of the Thanksgiving (i. 3–11) forbids us to suppose that there were such
in the Philippian Church. St. Paul was probably suffering
from them in Rome, and was anticipating their appearance
at Philippi. We must take into account the moods of an
imprisoned, highly sensitive, and often solitary man
(Jülicher).

the unclean dogs] A.V. omits the article ; it is a particular
class of ' dogs ' that is censured. Theodore, like Horace
(*obscenaeque canes*), and Dr. Pusey, condemns dogs for their
ἀναισχυντία : Ambrosiaster and Pelagius for their bark.
Döllinger said that dogs are the only animals that make a
noise for the sake of making it. But it may be doubted
whether St. Paul is here thinking of either shamelessness
or barking. Dogs are unclean animals to Orientals, and
the scavenger dogs in Eastern cities are generally diseased.

Hence ' dog ' was a common word of reproach. Chrysostom remarks that ' dogs ' was a common name for Gentiles ; these Judaizers are as offensive as heathen.

the wicked workers] Active in mischief, especially in the work of making converts, ' adulterating the word of God.' See on 2 Cor. ii. 17, xi. 13. Theodoret thinks that ' workers ' must refer to conduct rather than to doctrine.

self-mutilation] As a religious rite their circumcision was as worthless as the gashings of the prophets of Baal, about which the cognate verb κατετέμνοντο is used 1 Kings xviii. 25. Cf. Gal. v. 12 ; Lev. xxi. 5. For the play on words, of which St. Paul is fond (κατατομή, περιτομή), see on i. 25. Chrysostom and Theodoret suggest that these Judaizers tried to mutilate the Church, and hence the expression. But that is not the Apostle's meaning. Horace is nearer the truth with his contemptuous *curti Judaei. Sat.* I. ix. 70. See Suicer, II. 66, 67.*

3. I call it mutilation] This is implied in the γάρ, and the ἡμεῖς which precedes γάρ is very emphatic. Cf. Stephen's speech Acts vii. 51, which St. Paul heard ; also Rom. ii. 25 f. and Ezek xliv. 7.

we Christians] Not ' we missionaries,' as some interpret ἡμεῖς. The Jews prided themselves on their rite of circumcision and called the uncircumcised Gentiles ' dogs ' ; it is Jews who are ' the dogs,' and the true circumcision has passed to the Gentiles.

the true circumcision] Col. ii. 11 ; Deut. x. 16, xxx. 6 ; Jer. iv. 4.

by the Spirit of God] This is the better reading (Θεοῦ), rather than ' offer worship to God ' (Θεῷ), which is less strongly attested and throws a somewhat pointless emphasis on to ' God.' Christians worship God who is spirit with the help of His Spirit. " The Spirit, in this usage of Paul, is not to be regarded as equivalent to the mere influence of God. It includes an ontological as well as an ethical

* Wiclif gives the word a curious turn, rendering it ' division ' ; so also Tindale and Cranmer with ' dissension.'

element " (Moffat, *Paul and Paulinism*, p. 38).   See Burton,
Spirit, Soul, and Flesh, pp. 193–198, 201.

the true worship] The genuine service of spiritual devotion.
Λατρεία and λατρεύω, originally used of *hired* service, came
to be technical terms for *religious* worship, a ministry of
voluntary surrender.   See Westcott on Heb. ix. 4, x. 2,
and Swete on Rev. vii. 15.

have our boast] Cf. i. 26, ii. 16 (where, as here, A.V.
wrongly has 'rejoice').   The expression is Pauline ; over
fifty times, and elsewhere rare.   See Robertson and Plummer
on 1 Cor. i. 31.

external privileges] Although ἐν σαρκί applies primarily
to circumcision and ceremonial observances, yet it covers
physical origin, heredity and nationality as well.   Cf.
Ἰσραὴλ κατὰ σάρκα 1 Cor. x. 18.   See on i. 25 for πέποιθα
and note οὐκ, not μή, of a plain matter of fact.   Winer,
p. 609 ; Moulton, *Proleg.* p. 231.

4. although I myself] The ἐγώ is emphatic ; it is no
longer 'we.'   The Philippians, being Gentiles, could not
claim the external privileges which all Jews possessed,
whereas the Apostle could claim them to the full ; 2 Cor.
xi. 18–22 ; Rom. xi. 1 ; Acts xxiii. 3.   Just as the exhortation to humility was enforced by the example of Christ
(ii. 5–8), so the warning against Judaism is enforced by the
experiences of His Apostle.   'Might have' (A.V., R.V.)
is incorrect ; he did have.

even in these very privileges] 'Even' (R.V.) seems to
be the meaning of καί.   But it may mean 'also' (A.V.), in
these externals as well as in the privileges which belong to
Christians.   In either case it implies that they are hardly
worth mentioning.

if any other man] Some of the Judaizers would do so.

thinks] Cf. 1 Cor. iii. 18, viii. 2, x. 12 : not 'seems' ; cf.
2 Cor. x. 9 ; Gal. ii. 9.   Vulg. has *videtur*.   'Thinks' is
ironical.

I more securely] ' I have a stronger reason for such confidence.'   What follows is in substance very similar to 2 Cor.
xi. 22–28 ; but in expression the two differ considerably.

In both we have a precious fragment of autobiography,
drawn from him, like Newman's *Apologia*, by hostile criticism. The rejoinder in 2 Cor. is more vehement and
rhetorical in form. Here he states the points of comparison more calmly.

5. **on the eighth day**] Lit. ' For circumcision eight days
old '; cf. τεταρταῖος, Jn. xi. 39. This alone proved that
he was a Jew by birth (Gen. xvii. 12 ; Lev. xii. 3). Ishmaelites, like Ishmael (Gen. xvii. 25), were not circumcised
till they were thirteen years old. Proselytes might be any
age at the time of their circumcision. See Conybeare and
Howson, ch. II.

Israel] The name implies the covenant with God ; it is
the religious name of the nation. See on 2 Cor. xi. 22.
Ishmaelites claimed descent from Abraham, Edomites
from Abraham and Isaac, Israelites from Abraham, Isaac,
and Israel, the 'prince and wrestler with God.' For
ἐκ cf. Jn. iii. 1, 6, 31 ; Col. iv. 11.

tribe of Benjamin] Owing to the confusion caused by the
Captivity, by no means every Jew knew to what tribe he
belonged. The tribe of Benjamin was renowned as having
within its borders the Holy City, as having supplied Israel
with the first king, and as being the only tribe which remained faithful to Judah after the disruption of the kingdom. Cf. Ezra iv. 1.

Hebrew son] Lit. ' a Hebrew sprung from Hebrews.'
There was no heathen blood in him. Both his parents
were pure Jews. Though living out of Palestine they used
the Hebrew Scriptures and spoke Aramaic (Chrysostom,
Oecumenius, Theophylact). This late meaning of ' Hebrew,'
as specially referring to language, seems to prevail in N.T.
See Trench, § xxxix. ; Hastings, *DB*. II. p. 326, *DAC*. I.
p. 533. The names seem to be in a descending climax,
' Israel ' denoting the highest, and Hebrew the lowest,
of the distinctions.

The verse should have ended here. We now come to
distinctions which depended upon St. Paul's own will and
judgment. Here the climax, if there is one, ascends. Phari-

saism might be conventional ; persecution might be mere
ferocity ; punctilious fulfilment of the Law was at any rate
real.

As regards the law] Νόμον has no article, but evidently the
Jewish Law is meant. He took the Pharisees' view of it.
His father was a Pharisee (Acts xxiii. 6, xxvi. 5). But
' son of ' *may* mean ' disciple of.'

6. **Zeal for the national faith**] Gal. i. 14 ; Acts xxi. 20, xxii.
3–5 ; 1 Macc. ii. 58.

I persecuted] This had become a great shame to him, *le
sujet d'une douloureuse humiliation. Il s'en afflige comme
s'il avait persécuté le Seigneur lui-même* (Sabatier). But
he sarcastically states it here as being, in the eyes of many
Jews, a glorious distinction. Gal. i. 13 ; 1 Tim. i. 13.
He had persecuted, as the Jews are now persecuting him ;
and in each case the persecution was conscientious.

observance of the law] Again νόμος has no article,
although Jewish Law is meant. A.V. renders κατά in
three different ways, ' as touching,' ' concerning,' ' touching.' In the third clause it ignores γενόμενος.

showed myself] ' Came to be,' ' proved myself.'

blameless] Minute duties were scrupulously performed,
and no Pharisee, however strict, could have blamed him for
laxity. As regards *justitia externa literalis* he was *communi
hominum existimatione* faultless (Calvin). Cf. the rich young
man, Mt. xix. 20 ; Mk. x. 20.

7. **such things**] ' All that were of such a character as to
be gains ' ; ἅτινα ἦν κέρδη. See on ii. 20 and cf. Gal.
iv. 24. For ' these ' (ταῦτα) A.V. has ' those.'

in order to win Christ] ' For Christ ' (A.V., R.V.) is too
vague.

have set down] Abiding result of past action.

so much loss] On the credit side are entries which make
a show of value ; when properly estimated, they are not
only worthless, they represent a dead loss. The change
from plural (κέρδη) to singular (ζημίαν) marks the difference
between items and net result. See on iv. 14.

The Apostle again repeats himself, as in ii. 2. The repetition of the same words must be preserved in English; κέρδη. ἰκερδήσω—ἥγημαι, ἡγοῦμαι, ἡγοῦμαι—ζημίαν, ζημίαν, ἐζημιώθην—πάντα, τὰ πάντα—Χριστόν, Χριστοῦ, Χριστοῦ. The repetition is the effect of eagerness and earnestness.

8. **Nay,¹ moreover, I even**] We have an accumulation of particles, ἀλλὰ μὲν οὖν γε καί, or ἀλλὰ μὲν οὖν with or without καί (readings vary), the combined force of which seems to be to reinforce the previous statement. Winer, p. 552 ; Blass, § 77, 13, 14. He not only ' *has* set down *these* things ' just mentioned, but ' he *continues* to set down *all* things,' as a minus quality, as just so much loss.

when compared with] We have διά with the accusative thrice in *vv.* 7, 8. It is possible that in all three cases it means ' for the sake of,' ' in order to win.' But in this second case it seems to mean ' by reason of,' ' in consideration of,' which here is equivalent to ' in comparison with ' ; τῇ παραθέσει τῶν κρειττόνων (Theodoret).

the supreme value] 'The surpassingness.' For the neuter participle with the article followed by a genitive cf. Rom. ii. 4 ; Lk. ii. 27. A. T. Robertson, *Gr.* pp. 767, 1109 ; Blass, § 47, 1. Vulg. has a weak adjective ; *propter eminentem scientiam.* Better Beza ; *propter eminentiam cognitionis.*

Christ Jesus my Lord] With emphatic fullness at the end of the sentence. It indicates his own experience of the Jesus who as Christ was crucified and of the Lord who had appeared to him and in whom he had lived for years. See Hort on 1 Pet. i. 3.

I suffered the loss] At his conversion he was willing to have everything confiscated (2 Cor. vii. 9 ; Lk. ix. 25) without exception. Τὰ πάντα is stronger than the preceding πάντα. Cf. *v.* 21 ; Eph. i. 10, 11, iv. 15 ; also οἱ πάντες, ii. 21.*

utter refuse] 'Dogsmeat,' or ' dung.' The derivation of σκύβαλον is uncertain. It is used of what is thrown away as worthless or abominable, especially the refuse from a meal,

---

* Farrar suggests that his conversion may have involved the loss of all his means of living.

G

or excrement. Cf. the savourless salt, not fit even for the
dunghill, Lk. xiv. 35, and περικαθάρματα, 1 Cor. iv. 13 ;
also σκύβαλα ἀνθρώπου ἐν λογισμῷ αὐτοῦ, Ecclus. xxvii. 14.

gain Christ] So R.V., rather than ' *win Christ*,' as A.V.
We must keep to the commercial metaphor of balancing
accounts. Gain Christ now in the life.

9. **may be found**] On ' the Day of Jesus Christ ' (i. 6, 10,
ii. 16), when the great testing takes place : it is not a recogni-
tion by other Christians that is meant. ' Found ' in this
context suggests the outcome of a trial ; cf. ii. 8 and 2 Cor.
v. 3.

a member of] Lit. ' *in* Him.'

of my own] The adjectival pronouns (ἐμός, etc.) are
not used in N.T., unless emphatic, as here. Contrast ὑμῶν,
i. 19, 25, ii. 30. Simcox, *Language of N.T.* pp. 54 f.

from the law] From scrupulous observance of all its regu-
lations. As in vv. 6, 7 the Mosaic Law is meant. The
clauses form a chiasmus, ' through faith ' balancing ' from
the law,' and ' righteousness from God ' balancing ' righteousness of my own.' Chiasmus is frequent in Paul ; 1 Cor.
iii. 17, iv. 10, viii. 13, xiii. 2 ; 2 Cor. iv. 3, vi. 8, ix. 6, x. 12,
etc.

righteousness from God] See Thackeray, *St. Paul and
Jewish Thought*, pp. 85, 89.

this faith] The faith just mentioned, τῇ πίστει.

10. **know and appropriate**] Or, 'get to know and appreciate,'
τοῦ γνῶναι, which in construction depends on ἵνα κερδήσω.
Cf. Rom. vi. 6. A process is implied in γινώσκω, and the
knowledge is experimental and practical. The constr.
τοῦ with the infinitive is very frequent in Paul and Luke.

This implies] It is convenient to make a break in the long
Greek sentence.

the power] All that His resurrection implies and effects,
especially our rising from sin to a new life here, and our rising
to eternal life hereafter. " It reversed every doom of every
kind of death, and thus annulled the hopelessness which
must settle down on every one who thinks out seriously
what is involved in the universal empire of death. It was

by the faith in the Resurrection that mankind was enabled
to renew its youth " (Hort on 1 Pet. i. 4). Even more than
that ; " It was the guarantee of man's final attainment of
fullness of life " (Anon.). ' The power which raised Him '
is not the meaning.

fellowship in His sufferings] Closely coupled with ' the
power of His resurrection '; the two terms have only
one article. St. Paul is giving his own spiritual experiences,
and hence the order of the clauses. Christ's sufferings
preceded His resurrection ; but St. Paul recognized the risen
Christ before he participated in His sufferings. ' I will show
him how many things he must suffer for My Name's sake,'
Acts ix. 16. The fellowship includes the internal conflict
with temptation as well as the external conflict with
persecutors. See on 2 Cor. i. 5, iv. 10 ; and for κοινωνία on
ii. 1.

St. Paul's getting to know that Jesus Christ had risen
influenced the whole of his subsequent life ; Sanday and
Headlam on Rom. viii. 11, 34 ; Pfleiderer, *Paulinism*, pp. 169,
192. " Paul's religion was not an artificial creation but an
affair of real life . . . under the inspirations furnished by his
own immediate experience " (Case, *The Evolution of Christianity*, p. 354). Gwynn compares the second part of the
Exhortation in the Visitation of the Sick.

my nature conformed to] Transformed so as to share it.
With συμμορφιζόμενος here cf. συμμόρφους, Rom. viii. 29,
and μεταμορφούμεθα, 2 Cor. iii. 18 ; Rom. xii. 2 ; also the
sense, otherwise worded, of Rom. vi. 5 ; 2 Cor. iv. 10. See
Lightfoot, p. 130.

to His death] By the prospect of martyrdom. St. Paul
" here implies his expectation of death, to be followed by
resurrection ; not of survival till the Lord's Return "
(Moule).

11. if so be that I may attain] He states the matter
doubtfully, in humble admission of his own frailty and
unworthiness. For εἴ πως cf. Rom. i. 10, xi. 14 ; Acts xxvii.
12 ; Moulton, *Proleg.* pp. 187, 195 ; Burton, *Moods and
Tenses*, § 276 ; Blass, § 65, 6. Καταντᾶν is specially used of

reaching a *destination*. With the aorist subjunct. here cf. καταλάβω, v. 12 ; and see M. and M., *Vocabulary*, p. 183.

the rising again] The double compound ἐξανάστασις occurs nowhere in LXX and nowhere else in N.T., and in translation the difference from ἀνάστασις should be marked, although there is no difference in meaning. In late Greek, compounds become very frequent. Bengel refines too much when he suggests that ἀνάστασις refers to Christ and ἐξανάστασις to Christians. M. and M., p. 221.

from the dead] Throughout his Epistles, St. Paul has in his mind ' those who are in the way of salvation ' (οἱ σωζόμενοι) far more often than ' those who are on the way to perdition ' (οἱ ἀπολλύμενοι). He has the former in mind here ; and possibly for that reason says ' *from* the dead ' rather than ' *of* the dead.' They are freed once and for ever from the category of ' the dead.' The theory of two resurrections, one of the righteous and another of the remainder, is to be regarded with great caution. In 1 Thess. iv. 16 ' rise first ' means ' rise at once,' before the Christians who are alive are caught up into the air. See Swete's full note on Rev. xx. 5.

iii. 12–21. WARNING AGAINST ANTINOMIANISM.

The drift of the whole section is clear. Freedom from Judaism, which relies so much on external conformity to law, implies no encouragement to laxity of life. The details are less clear. Laxity of life seems to be contemplated under two forms, the delusion that perfection has been already attained (12–16), and the delusion that Christian liberty involves the abolition of all moral restraints (17–21). In both cases, as in the preceding section (2–11), the Apostle points to his own spiritual experiences, and the connexion between v. 11 and v. 12 is close.

12–16. None of us is really perfect.

[12] Not as though I had already attained, either were already perfect : but I follow after, if that I may apprehend that for which also I am apprehended of Christ Jesus. [13] Brethren, I count not myself to have apprehended : but this one thing *I do*, forgetting

those things which are behind, and reaching forth unto those things which are before, ¹⁴ I press toward the mark, for the prize of the high calling of God in Christ Jesus.   ¹⁵ Let us, therefore, as many as be perfect, be thus minded : and if in any thing ye be otherwise minded, God shall reveal even this unto you.   ¹⁶ Nevertheless, where-unto we have already attained, let us walk by the same rule, let us mind the same thing.

It is worth while to show the close connexion between the end of the first Warning and the beginning of the second.

¹² Mark my ' if so be.'   I do not mean that by my conversion I did already reach the goal, nor do I claim, as some do, that I am already made perfect.   Not so.   I am pressing forward in the race to see if I may really grasp the prize, encouraged to do this because I was really grasped by Christ.   ¹³ Brethren, whatever others may think about themselves, I for one do not account myself to have grasped the prize.   My one rule of conduct is this.   Forgetting both the failures and the successes which lie behind me, and straining after what still lies in front, ¹⁴ I am pressing forward towards the goal, to win the prize, which is no less than God's invitation in Christ Jesus to enter into the joys of heaven.   ¹⁵ Let those of us therefore who may consider that they are already perfect in the Christian life be thus minded as regards the need for strenuous effort.   Hold that principle fast, and then, if in any particular you are differently minded from me, this also God will reveal to you as He has to me.   ¹⁶ Only, whatever truth we have reached, by the same we must direct our steps.

12. **I do not mean**] See on iv. 11.

already made perfect] This would not happen till his life on earth was completed.   See Westcott on Heb. xii. 23.

I did already reach] The aorist ἔλαβον may indicate a definite point of time in the past ; and if so, his conversion, which he has just described (*vv.* 7 f.), is probably meant. The aorist may also refer to his life regarded as a whole ; ' I do not mean that I have reached the goal.'   There are cases in which it is the Greek idiom to use the aorist where we in English use the perfect ; and then to translate the Greek aorist by the English aorist is misleading.   Here, as in Jn. viii. 29, the interpretation is doubtful, and therefore the rendering is doubtful.   In Jn. xiii. 13, 34, xv. 9, 12, we must have the perfect in English.

A.V. has 'attain' for both καταντήσω and ἔλαβον.

I am pressing forward . . . really grasp] Lit. 'I pursue . . . catch.' For διώκω see on 1 Thess. v. 15. Of the alternative renderings, 'press forward' and 'pursue' or 'follow after' (Rom. ix. 30, xii. 13), either makes good sense here; but 'press forward' is necessary in v. 14 and therefore better here. Strenuous effort is implied. For καταλαμβάνω see Cor. ix. 24; for εἰ with the subjunctive, v. 11; 1 Cor. xiv. 5; Blass, § 65, 6; A. T. Robertson, *Gr.* pp. 934, 1017, 1044. The play on words between ἔλαβον and καταλάβω might be reproduced with 'take' and 'take hold.' The former implies receiving a gift, the latter grasping a prize.

because] Ἐφ' ᾧ is often ambiguous. Here, as in 2 Cor. v. 4, 'because' seems to be preferable to 'wherefore.' We might render 'that for which' (A.V.), viz. his future salvation; but 'because' is better.

grasped by Christ] As a prize, on the way to Damascus. Everywhere he regards his conversion as a sudden and supernatural thing : he was not gradually led from Judaism to Christianity. Knowling, *Testimony of St. Paul to Christ*, pp. 188 f.

13. Brethren] The address introduces an important statement ; here to correct a possible misapprehension ; cf. 1 Thess. v. 25 ; Rom. x. 1 ; Gal. iii. 15, vi. 1. In such cases ἀδελφοί stands first in the sentence.

I for one] The emphatic position of ἐγὼ ἐμαυτόν rather implies that there are some people who have a different opinion respecting themselves, or (less probably) a different opinion respecting him. Cf. Jn. v. 30, 31, vii. 17, etc. He is thinking of the Antinomians of vv. 18, 19.

do not account] The commercial metaphor again, as in vv. 7, 8, iv. 8. Λογίζομαι is exceedingly frequent in Paul, especially in Rom. and 2 Cor. A.V. has 'count' for both ἡγοῦμαι and λογίζομαι.

My one rule] There are various ways of expanding the elliptical ἓν δέ. If ἕν is accusative, 'But one thing I reckon,' or 'I do,' or 'I can say.' Such ellipses are not rare in the Epistles. A. T. Robertson, *Gr.* p. 391.

Forgetting, etc.] ' I let the dead past bury its own dead.'
He is neither despondent because of falls nor presumptuous
because of advances. 'Remember Lot's wife.' See Lk.
ix. 62 ; Mk. xiii. 16 ; Jn. vi. 66.

* **Straining after**] As in a footrace, which is one of St. Paul's
favourite metaphors. Double prepositional compounds
like ἀπεκτεινόμενος here and ἀπεκδεχόμεθα, v. 20, become
very common in late Greek. A. T. Robertson, *Gr.* p. 165.
Although he owes all to God, yet he is responsible for the
use which he makes of Divine grace. Footrace (ii. 16) is
more probable than chariot-race (Farrar).

14. **the goal**] Or ' the mark ' (σκοπόν), that on which one
fixes one's gaze ; in shooting, the target (Job xvi. 13 ; Lam.
iii. 12), in racing, the goal. The runner *pursues* it, as something to come down on or overtake, κατὰ σκοπὸν διώκει.

to win the prize] Lit. ' unto the prize,' which is awaiting
the winner at the goal. Cf. 1 Cor. ix. 24, 25. The derivation of βραβεῖον is unknown ; it occurs Clem. Rom. *Cor.*
v. 5, and is frequent in papyri.

God's invitation ... heaven] Lit. ' the upward calling
of God.' Κλῆσις is used of invitations to a banquet, and in
N.T. often of the Divine invitation to enter the Kingdom ;
Rom. xi. 29. This Divine invitation is perpetual, and it is
ἄνω in its action and in its result. Cf. Rom. viii. 30 ; 1 Cor.
i. 26, vii. 20 ; Heb. iii. 1 ; Pet. i. 12. Chrysostom
says that athletes are not crowned in the race-course
below ; the king calls them *up* and *there* crowns them.
He takes ' in Christ Jesus ' with ' am pressing forward ' :
but see 1 Cor. vii. 22 ; 1 Pet. v. 10 ; Clem. Rom. *Cor.* xlvi. 6.

15. **perfect**] Probably there is irony in the Apostle's
placing himself, hypothetically, among such people, as in
1 Cor. viii. 1. Some Corinthians had claimed special
knowledge, and some among the Philippians had claimed
to be ' perfect.' " Christian perfection really consists
only in this constant striving for perfection " (B. Weiss).
See also Gregory of Nyssa, *adv. Eunomium,* VIII. 5, *sub fin.,*
and Pfleiderer, *Paulinism,* I. p. 225.

are differently minded] With regard to the question

of perfection and the duty of pressing forward. Ἑτέρως occurs nowhere else in N.T. It probably suggests erroneous, but not heretical teaching. See on 2 Cor. xi. 4.

this also] viz. ' that in which you are differently minded.' ' Even this ' (A.V., R.V.) is less suitable. Calvin remarks that *nemo ita loqui jure posset, nisi cui certa constat suae doctrinae ratio.* Cf. Eph. iii. 3.

will reveal to you] Emphasis on ' you.' ' God has granted a revelation to correct my erroneous convictions ; if necessary, He will do the like for you.'

16. **Only**] The verse is elliptical and somewhat obscure. The Greek gives ' Only whereunto we reached, in the same to walk.' The infinitive is a strong imperative, as in Rom. xii. 15 and Titus ii. 2–10. This imperatival infinitive was often used in laws and maxims, and it is found in papyri. Perhaps ' we must ' or ' we are bound to ' is to be understood. Burton, § 364 ; Moulton, *Proleg.* p. 179. What is it that ' we reached ' ? Probably the principle that we must never cease striving to make advance ; our present position must be only a means to further progress, step by step : *travaillons sans relâche, et ne croyons jamais que c'est assez.* Cf. Rom. iv. 12.

The insertion of ' rule ' with ' the same ' and the addition of ' mind the same thing ' are interpolations from Gal. vi. 16 and from Phil. ii. 4 respectively.

17–21. No one has licence to sin.

[17] Brethren, be followers together of me, and mark them which walk so as ye have us for an ensample. [18] (For many walk, of whom I have told you often, and now tell you even weeping, *that they are* the enemies of the cross of Christ : [19] Whose end *is* destruction, whose God *is* their belly, and whose glory *is* in their shame, who mind earthly things.) [20] For our conversation is in heaven, from whence also we look for the Saviour, the Lord Jesus Christ : [21] Who shall change our vile body, that it may be fashioned like unto his glorious body, according to the working whereby he is able even to subdue all things unto himself.

Once more the Apostle appeals to experience. The Philippians know his manner of life and that of his fellow

missionaries.   Has their conduct ever given any encouragement to moral laxity ?

[17] Be united, one and all of you, Brethren, in becoming imitators of
me ; and carefully regard as your aim those whose walk in life is so
fashioned that you have me and my colleagues as a pattern.   [18] This
is no needless caution ; for there are many, of whom I many times
used to tell you, and now tell you even with tears, that they walk in
life as the enemies of the cross of Christ.   [19] Their end is perdition ;
sensual indulgence is their god ; their glory is in what is really
their shame, they whose minds grovel in earthly things.   [20] Such men
have no fellowship with us Christians.   For our real home and country
is not on earth, but in heaven ; and it is from heaven that we confidently look for a Saviour also, even the Lord Jesus Christ.   [21] He
will change the passing fashion of this body of ours—the body of our
temporary humiliation, so as to share the lasting form of His own body
—the body of His eternal glory.   He will do this by the working
of the Divine power which enables Him even to bring into subjection
to Himself all things alike.

17. **Be united, etc.**] This is probably the meaning of
συνμιμηταί μου γίνεσθε :   omnes uno consensu et una mente
(Calvin).   Some interpret the συν- as meaning ' join with me
in imitating,' i.e. in imitating Christ.   But what follows
shows that the Apostle is here giving himself as a pattern.
' Be united with *others* who imitate me ' is possible, but
it gives συν- an unnatural meaning.   See on 1 Thess. i. 6 ; 2
Thess. iii. 7, 9 ; 1 Cor. iv. 16, xi. 1.   ' Followers ' (A.V.
habitually for μιμηταί) is inadequate.

regard as your aim] As in *v.* 4.   Contrast βλέπετε in *v.* 2.
*Cogita, quantum nobis exempla bona prosint: scies mag-
norum virorum non minus praesentia esse utilem memoriam*
(Seneca, *Ep.* cii. 30).

those whose walk] Presumably their pastors.

me and my colleagues] ' Me ' is felt to be egotistical, and
' us ' is substituted.   It includes Silas, Timothy, and
others who had worked with St. Paul at Philippi.   As in
2 Thess. iii. 9, we have τύπον, not τύπους.   It is the missionaries collectively who supply the pattern.   They have
started a Christian tradition, which by its variety in detail
shows that the Christian life is possible for all.   For τύπον

ἡμᾶς Codices Amiatinus and Fuldensis have *formam nos*,
while Vulg. and other Latin authorities have the obviously
corrupt *formam nostram*.

18. **for there are many**] The charge to imitate their
teachers requires explanation, and it at once receives it.
The evil is widespread, of long standing, and grave. It
probably existed among Roman Christians, although not
as yet at Philippi, as the high praise in the Thanksgiving
(i. 3–8) shows. But it might spread thither, and was already
discussed there. He mentions no names of persons either
at Rome or elsewhere : personal denunciation might do
more harm than good.

many times used to tell] We perhaps might render, ' whom
I many times used to call in your hearing, the enemies, etc.' *
Such reiteration was absolutely necessary, as all missionaries
know, where converts from heathenism live in heathen
surroundings. Hort thinks that he is still denouncing the
Judaizers rather than teachers of antinomian principles
(*Judaistic Christianity*, p. 115). The language is too
general for certainty. It was the Judaizers who said that
St. Paul's teaching about the Law led to generally lawless
conduct.

even with tears] Tears for their miserable condition, as
well as for his own suffering. Cf. Lk. xix. 41 ; 2 Cor. ii. 4 ;
Acts xx. 31. Like J. H. Newman, while writing the
Apologia pro Vita sua in 1864 ; " I have been constantly
in tears, and constantly crying out in distress " (Letter to
Hope Scott, 2 May). These sinners perhaps had said that
they were carrying out the Apostle's own teaching about
freedom from the Law.

the enemies of the cross] Those who were specially such.
The expression illustrates the emphasis which St. Paul
placed on the cross,—to him the symbol of self-renunciation,
but to the heathen, of foolishness and horror ; 1 Cor. i.
18, 23. These men mocked the cross by gross self-indulg-
ence.

19. **Their end is perdition**] ' The end ' which follows from

* Note the play between πολλοί and πολλάκις.

such conduct ; he proceeds to explain why. ' Perdition '
not ' destruction ' (A.V.). Cf. Rom. i. 21 ; v. 32, viii. 13 ;
2 Cor. xi. 15 ; Gal. vi. 8 ; Jas. i. 15 ; 2 Pet. ii. 1–3. *Que
l'on pèche impunément, c'est le comble du désordre ; ce
serait le désordre, non de l'homme qui pèche, mais de Dieu
qui ne punit pas* (Bossuet).

sensual indulgence] Here, and perhaps Rom. xvi. 18,
' the belly ' (κοιλία) means the fleshly appetites generally,
as in Ecclus. xxiii. 6. 'Mere selfishness seems to be inadequate. P. Ewald compares γαστρὶ δουλεύειν, γαστρίδουλος,
κοιλιόδουλος, κοιλιολάτρης : add κοιλιοδαίμων. See Suicer,
II. 119.* This hardly applies to Judaizers.

their glory, etc.] Their boasted liberty was shameful
slavery to lust. As Père Hyacinthe said to a company of
' free-thinkers ' at Cannes ; " *Vous êtes ni libres ni pen-
seurs ; vous étes les esclaves de vos préjugés, de vos passions,
de vos péchés.*"

earthly things] Col. iii. 2 ; Jas. iii. 15. This seems almost
a bathos after the three strong statements which precede it.
But it prepares the way for the magnificent contrast which
follows in *vv.* 20, 21, in which Way finds material for another
hymn : " Hymn of the Citizens of Heaven."

20. **For our real**] ' For ' and the emphatic ' our ' imply
absolute rejection of such misinterpretation of freedom.

country and home] ' Conversation '=' daily life ' (A.V.)
is now misleading. ' Citizenship ' (R.V.) or ' common-
wealth ' (R.V. marg.) are better renderings of πολίτευμα,
which also means ' citizen-life ' or ' citizen-duties '; but the
local sense seems to be required by ἐξ οὗ. Tertullian and
Jerome have *municipatus*. This heavenly Fatherland
is the home of the highest moral liberty, and is in emphatic
contrast to ' earthly things.' Cf. Eph. ii. 19 ; Heb. xi. 13.
Plato has a remarkable parallel, *Rep.* ix. p. 592 B ; also

---

* *Aspice, quemadmodum immensae hominum cupiditates hient
semper et poscant. Alius libidine insanit, alius abdomini servit,
alius lucri totus est* (Seneca, De Benef. VII. xxvi. 3). *Quid mihi
voluptatem nominas ? Hominis bonum quaero, non ventris* (De
Vita Beata, ix. 3).

Philo, *De Confus.* i. 416 Mang. The description of Christians in the Epistle to Diognetus v. 9, ἐπὶ γῆς διατρίβουσιν ἀλλ᾽ ἐν οὐράνῳ πολιτεύονται,, may be an echo of this passage. Cf. ' Where your treasure is, etc.,' and see F. B. Westcott, *A Letter from Asia*, p. 138.

is in heaven] Not ἐστι, but ὑπάρχει, and hence the insertion of ' real.' It is no Utopia ; it exists. It is now ; not will be hereafter. And it is ours already. See on ii. 6 and 2 Cor. viii. 17, xii. 16 ; cf. Gal. iv. 26 ; Heb. xii. 22.

we confidently look for] The ' we ' may include the departed as well as those who are in this world. In the strong compound ἀπεκδεχόμεθα the ἀπο implies disregard of other things and concentration on one object, as in ἀποκαραδοκία, i. 20. Cf. Rom. viii. 19 ; 1 Cor. i. 7 ; Heb. ix. 28. It seems to have been a usual word for expressing expectation of the Advent. Its use in 1 Pet. iii. 2 and in Heb. ix. 28 may have come from St. Paul, who may possibly have coined the word. M. and M., *Vocabulary*, p. 56.

a Saviour] The word is emphatic ; ' And it is from heaven that as a *Saviour* also we look for, etc.' It probably comes from LXX : but its connexion with πολίτευμα here makes an allusion to the pagan use of the word to designate the Emperor not improbable. With the exception of Luke, the title in N.T. is found only in the later writings. In the Pastoral Epistles and in 2 Peter it is frequent.

the Lord Jesus Christ] He is the Lord of the heavenly πολίτευμα. See on *v.* 8 for similarly emphatic fullness.

21. change the passing fashion] In the compounds μετασχηματίσει and σύμμορφον we must again mark the radical difference between σχῆμα and μορφή, as in ii. 6–8. The one is external and transitory, the other is essential and permanent. Vulg. has *reformabit, configuratum,* which just spoils the Old Latin *transfigurabit, conformatum.* Cf. 2 Cor. xi. 13–15.

But ' vile body ' (A.V.) is misleading, like Luther's *unsern nichtigen Leib,* and Beza's *corpus nostrum humile.* There is here no trace of the Gnostic view that everything material is

impure, and that the human body is an object of contempt.
As compared with the spiritual body in the future life,
it is in a condition of humiliation. Those who share the
humiliation of Christ (ii. 8) may hope to share His glory
(ii. 9). Cf. Rom. i. 4 and see Hort on 1 Pet. i. 21. There may
be a secondary argument against those who make indulgence
of the body their aim in life,—a body which will soon be re-
fashioned. ' Body ' (not ' bodies ') is generic, as in Rom.
vi. 12.

body of His eternal glory] ' His glorious body ' (A.V.) is
weak and inadequate. Neither here nor 2 Cor. iv. 4 nor
Rom. viii. 21 is τῆς δόξης a characterizing genitive. ' The
glory ' is that in which He appeared to St. Paul.

working] Excepting 2 Thess. ii. 9, 11, ἐνέργεια in N.T.
is always used of Divine activity ; there of diabolical.
All instances therefore are of *supernatural* energy, and all
are in the writings of St. Paul (Eph. i. 19, iii. 7, iv. 16 ; Col.
i. 29, ii. 12), and are characteristic of our group. M. and
M., *Vocabulary*, p. 214.

which enables Him] The construction (τοῦ *c. infin.*)
is very frequent in Paul and Luke. Blass, § 71, 3.

to Himself] Strong testimony to His Divine power.*

all things alike] At the close, with emphasis. As in
v. 8, πάντα has the article ; there are no exceptions, not
even death ; 1 Cor. xv. 25–27. There may be an allusion
to Ps. viii. 6.

iv. 1–9.   RENEWED EXHORTATIONS

Somewhat like iii. 1, iv. 1 is isolated, and may be called
transitional. The long digression which begins suddenly,
through some cause unknown to us, has come to an end with
the solemn words in iii. 20, 21. This verse springs naturally
out of the previous warnings, as ὥστε shows. Equally

---

* αὐτῷ, not ἑαυτῷ, is the right reading, but it certainly looks
back to ὅς, and therefore to ' the Lord Jesus Christ.' If αὐτῷ be
adopted, it is a unique feature in N.T.

naturally it leads on to more specific exhortations as to the
necessity of unity and concord (2, 3),less definite exhortations
in the same direction having been given i. 27–ii. 18.

¹ Therefore, my brethren, dearly beloved and longed for, my
joy and crown, so stand fast in the Lord, my dearly beloved.

It is necessary to show the connexion with what precedes
and what follows.

¹ So then, remembering that you are citizens of a heavenly kingdom
and are earnestly expecting a heavenly Saviour, listen to my renewed
appeal. You are my brethren, whom I love and long to see again,
you are my present joy and the crown which I hope to win. For
all these reasons stand fast in the Lord, my beloved ones, and show
your steadfastness by inward union.

1. So then] For ὥστε introducing the result of what has
just been stated, and followed by an imperative, cf. ii. 12 ;
1 Thess. iv. 18 ; 1 Cor. iii. 21, etc. Outside the Pauline
Epistles the combination is rare. T. A. Robertson, *Gr.* p. 999.

my brethren, whom I love, etc.] It is a relief to turn
from the enemies of the Cross to the affectionate and
generous Philippians. In his earnestness the Apostle
accumulates words of affection, and (as in ii. 2) is careless
about repetition. Nowhere else does he use this full form
of address : *blandis appellationibus . . . quae tamen non
sunt adulationis, sed sinceri amoris* (Calvin).

long to see again] Ἐπιπόθητος occurs nowhere else
in N.T. or in LXX, but ἐπιποθεῖν is in all four of the
Pauline groups ; i. 8, ii. 26 ; 1 Thess. iii. 6 ; etc. We have
ἐπιπόθησις, 2 Cor. vii. 7, 11, and ἐπιποθεία, Rom. xv. 23.

crown] Here, as in 1 Thess. ii. 19, the ' crown ' (στέφανος)
is the wreath or garland worn as a mark of success or desert
(1 Cor. ix. 25). The Philippians will be such a crown at the
Day of Judgment to the Apostle who converted them and
established them in the faith. *   This shows that no Philip-

* *Saint Paul disait aux Philippiens qu'ils étaient sa couronne.
Ne pouvons-nous pas dire que nous sommes la couronne de Jésus-
Christ, mais une couronne de souffrances ? Il attendait que de nos
bonnes œuvres nous lui fissions une couronnes d'honneur, et par nos
iniquités nous lui en faisons une d'ignominie* (Bourdaloue).

pians are among those who are condemned in iii. 18, 19. See Ropes, on Jas. i. 12 ; Hastings, *DB*. art. ' Crown ' ; Trench, *Syn*. § xxiii.

For all these reasons] ' According to my instructions and exhortations ' seems to be the meaning of οὕτως. It commonly refers to what precedes. See on Thess. iv. 17. **stand fast**] See on i. 27 and cf. 1 Thess. iii. 8 ; ' in the Lord ' is certainly not to be taken with ' my beloved ones.'

iv. 2, 3. EXHORTATION TO UNITY.

2 I beseech Euodias, and beseech Syntyche, that they be of the same mind in the Lord. 3 And I intreat thee also, true yokefellow, help those women which laboured with me in the Gospel, with Clement also, and with other my fellow-labourers, whose names are in the book of life.

These two verses raise several questions which cannot be answered with any certainty. (1) What was the nature of the controversy between the two first mentioned ? (2) Is either of the two to be identified with the Lydia of Acts xvi. 14, 15 ? (3) Is the word rendered ' yokefellow ' a proper name ? If not, who is this yokefellow ? Some other questions may be answered with confidence. Are the first names names of real persons, or do they represent parties in the Church ? Beyond reasonable doubt they are names of persons, both of whom are women. Does ' yoke-fellow ' mean the Apostle's wife ? Assuredly not, but the hypothesis is ancient, and as such requires notice.

2 I exhort Euodia, and I exhort Syntyche, to put an end to their differences and be of the same mind in the Lord. 3 Yes, and I ask thee also as a friend, my genuine and faithful yokefellow, to give these two ladies a helping hand towards reconciliation and reunion, for they were united in fighting side by side with me in my contests on behalf of the Gospel ; along with Clement also and the rest of my fellow workers, whose names, although I mention them not, are enrolled in the Book of Life.

2. **I exhort**] The context decides whether παρακαλεῖν, which is frequent in N.T., means ' exhort,' ' encourage ' or

' console.' It does not occur in any of the Johannine books, or in Jas. or 2 Pet.

Euodia] A.V. makes Εὐοδίαν the acc. of a man's name, Euodias ; but no such name has been found. Euodia or Euhodia is fairly frequent in inscriptions, and no doubt this is right here as the name of some Philippian lady.

Syntyche] Some propose to make Συντύχην the acc. of a man's name ; but no such name has been found, whereas Syntyche, Sintyche, and Suntyche do occur.* The αὐταῖς αἵτινες in v. 3 is conclusive as to both names being feminine. They were evidently well-known women in the Philippian Church, and exercised the liberty and influence which was common among Macedonian women at this time ; and in Macedonia women seem to have had a better social position than anywhere else in the civilized world. Acts xvi. 14, 40, xvii. 4, 12 give evidence of this ; and this feature is found also in inscriptions. The conjecture that ' Lydia ' in Acts xvi. 14, 40 means that she was a woman of Lydia, and that she may be identified with either Euodia or Syntyche, cannot be disproved, but it is not very probable. The quarrel between the two women was evidently notorious, and was leading to party spirit in the Church. That they were deaconesses is possible, and Renan treats the hypothesis as certain. ' I exhort ' with both names emphasizes the fact that the two persons are at present alienated from one another, and at the same time shows that the Apostle takes sides with neither. Both are in fault, and he makes the same appeal to both. *Hoc his ponit, quasi coram adhortans seorsum utramvis, idque summa cum acquitate* (Bengel).

be of the same mind] The same phrase as in ii. 2. The meaning here may be " agreement for the accomplishment of practical aims " (Zahn).

in the Lord] They are both of them members of Christ,

* Meyer attributes to Theodore of Mopsuestia the view that Syntyches was Euodia's husband. Theodore states that some people said so (τινες δέ φασιν). He himself suggests that the two ladies contended περὶ πρωτείων, *super primatum.*

as he is; i. 14, ii. 19, 24, 29, iii. 1, etc. They are sisters in Christ and ought not to be estranged.

3. **Yes**] Not ' And,' as A.V., following the corrupt reading καί for ναί. Ναί (*dulcis particula*) confirms, often a statement, sometimes an entreaty, as here and Philem. 20. Judith ix. 12 it is repeated. See Ellicott.

I ask as a friend] Only in his letters to the beloved Macedonian Churches does St. Paul use the more friendly ἐρωτῶ (1 Thess. iv. 1, v. 12 ; 2 Thess. ii. 1), which rather implies that the two parties are equal ; whereas ' exhort ' assumes some kind of authority over those who are exhorted. The change of word is remarkable. He gives what is almost a command to Euodia and Syntyche ; of his colleague he asks a favour. In classical Greek ἐρωτῶ is used of asking questions rather than of asking favours. In pre-Christian letters the two verbs are sometimes combined, as in 1 Thess. iv. 1. Trench, § xl. ; M. and M., p. 255.

genuine and faithful] Γνήσιος, as 1 Tim. i. 2 ; Tit. i. 4 ; 2 Cor. viii. 8, and nowhere else in N.T. See on γνησίως ii. 20 and cf. Ecclus vii. 18. The suggestion that it is a proper name, ' Gnesius, my fellow-worker,' may be disregarded. M. and M., *Vocabulary*, p. 129. Oddly enough, the Latin rendering, *germane compar*, led to the idea that *Germanus* was a proper name, which got into the Greek text of Cod. G.

yokefellow] Σύνζυγος from συνζεύγνυμι, ' I fasten together.' Some suggest that *this* is a proper name, and that γνήσιε points to its being so ; ' I ask Synzygus, rightly so called, a genuine yokefellow.' If so, we may compare the play on the name Onesimus in Philem. 11, and on Nabal in 1 Sam. xxv. 25. The objection that the name occurs nowhere else in literature or inscriptions is serious, but it does not prove that there could not have been a Philippian with such a name. We may compare this problem with 2 Jn. 1, where some render the ' elect lady ' as the ' elect Kyria,' and others as the ' lady Electa.'

Assuming that ' yokefellow ' is right, who is he ? Barnabas, Silas, Timothy, Luke, and the leading ' bishop ' in Philippi are conjectures. Victorinus suggests that the

H

Apostle now turns aside and addresses Epaphroditus,
who is to carry the letter, and is here urged to use his
personal influence ; and this view is adopted by Lightfoot,
Zahn, and others.   But was Epaphroditus to read this
about himself to the Philippians ?   Clement of Alexandria
and Origen mention an early belief that the ' yokefellow '
was the Apostle's wife, a belief which Chrysostom corrects.
Renan (S. Paul, p. 148) translates ma chère épouse, and
suggests Lydia, whom Baring Gould also thinks that the
Apostle may have married.   But he was unmarried or a
widower when he wrote 1 Cor. vii. 8, and if the yokefellow
was a woman we should have γνησία not γνήσιε, as Theodore
of Mopsuestia points out.   Wieseler (Chronologie, p. 548)
suggests Christ as the yokefellow !   In Hastings, DAC.
art. ' Synzygus,' it is assumed that the word is a proper
name.   WH. have σύνζυγε in their text, and Σύνζυγε in
the margin.   Ramsay adopts σύνζυγε as probably meaning
St. Luke.

   lend them a helping hand] Συνλαμβάνου αὐταῖς, mid.
voice with dative, as Lk. v. 7.   ' Lay hold of the difficulty
along with them.'

   for they were united] There is possibly a play on words
between συνλαμβάνου and συνήθλησαν.   There is certainly
a play of meaning between ' help them to unite now ' and
' for they were united before.'   Women were the first
hearers at Philippi ; Acts xvi. 13, 14.   " Lest their public
exhortation should appear to degrade these two women
before the congregation, Paul recalls the services which
they had rendered to the congregation ; and in order that
it might be known what events he had in mind, he mentions
the name of a man who also assisted him on that occasion "
(B. Weiss ad loc.).

   ' Help those women who ' (A.V.) mistranslates both αὐταῖς
and αἵτινες.   The latter gives the reason why they deserve
to be helped ; cf. i. 28, ii. 20 ; iii. 7 ; Gal. iv. 24, 26.

   fighting side by side with me] The favourite metaphor
from the arena ; i. 27, 30, ii. 16, iii. 13, 14.   ' Laboured
with me ' (A.V., R.V.) is inadequate.

along with Clement also] This looks back to ' fighting side by side with me ' rather than to ' give a helping hand.' He is mentioned because of his connexion with the two ladies. Clement is some Philippian about whom we know nothing. Gwynn's attempt to justify the patristic identification of this Clement with the famous bishop of Rome, third from Linus, and writer of the Roman Epistle to the Corinthians, is surprising. There is no evidence that this Clement ever migrated to Rome ; and, if he did, it is improbable that a Philippian would become the leading presbyter in the Roman Church. The name Clement was exceedingly common.* The καί before Κλήμεντος may be either ' also,' looking back to the two ladies, or ' both,' anticipating 'and the rest of my fellow-workers.' Hastings, *DB*. art. ' Clement.'

Book of Life] The metaphor is frequent in O.T. and in the Apocalypse ; Exod. xxxii. 32 ; 1 Sam. xxv. 29 ; Ps. lxix. 28, cxxxix. 16 ; Dan. xii. 1 ; etc. Rev. iii. 5, xiii. 8, xxi. 27, xxii. 19. See Swete on Rev. iii. 5 ; Charles on Enoch xlvii. 3 ; Hastings, *DAC*. art. ' Book of Life.' Wetstein gives illustrations from Rabbinical writers. The expression involves no doctrine of predestination. And it does not imply that these persons are dead ; Lk. x. 20.

iv. 4–7. RENEWED EXHORTATION TO JOY.

⁴ Rejoice in the Lord alway : and again I say, Rejoice. ⁵ Let your moderation be known unto all men. The Lord is at hand. ⁶ Be careful for nothing : but in everything by prayer and supplication with thanksgiving let your request be made known unto God. ⁷ And the peace of God, which passeth all understanding, shall keep your hearts and minds through Christ Jesus.

After the very brief and very gentle expression of dissatisfaction, the Apostle returns to the dominant note of

---

* Among the many inscriptions found in or near Philippi is a list of members of some guild or club. The last of the sixty-nine names is Valerius Clemens. Clement of Rome gives no hint in his Epistle that he stood in the relation to St. Paul which is indicated here— rather the contrary.

joyfulness. As in ch. iii. we had first religion (5–10) and then morality (17–21), so here (4–7 and 8, 9).

⁴ I have called you my joy. You yourselves must have joy on all occasions, as all Christians should. I can never say it too often, and I will say it yet again, Have joy.   ⁵ Let your forbearing spirit, not your contentiousness, become known to all men. The Lord, who will judge all self-assertion and strife, is at hand.   ⁶ In no case spoil your lives with needless anxieties ; but in every case, by your prayer and your supplication, always combined with thanksgiving, let your requests be made known before God.   ⁷ Then the peace which God gives in answer to prayer, which will calm your dissensions and forebodings, and which is more potent than self-assertion or brooding care, will keep guard over your debating hearts and your anxious minds, in Christ Jesus, who is your house of defence and your castle.

4. **have joy**] It is debated whether χαίρετε here means ‘ rejoice,’ as in ii. 18 ; 1 Thess. v. 16 ; Mt. v. 12 ; Lk. x. 20, or ‘ farewell,’ as in 2 Cor. xiii. 11, or something of both meanings, as perhaps in iii. 1. Vulg. here has *gaudete*, and of the two meanings it is manifest that ‘ rejoice ’ cannot well be excluded, because joy is such a prominent feature in the letter, and has just come to the front again in iv. 1. Here, as in 1 Thess. v. 16, 17, it is closely followed by an exhortation to cultivate the spirit of prayer as a security for joy. It is ‘ in the Lord,’ in the thought that we are one with Him, that joy can be secured (Chrysostom). Weinel (*St. Paul*, p. 125) says of these verses, " Here we have the key-note of the Christian life, as Paul conceived it. Like rays of bright sunshine, such words break forth from the heavy masses of Pauline polemics." See the parallel in Hab. iii. 17–19 ; also Is. xli. 16, lxi. 10.*

on all occasions] As in i. 4, 20, iii. 22, and generally in N.T., πάντοτε, not ἀεί. Cf. πάντοτε χαίρετε, 1 Thess. v. 16,

---

* Farrar points out how the joy of St. Paul during long imprisonment contrasts with the dismal despondency of Ovid in the *Tristia*, of Cicero in his letters from exile, and of Seneca in his treatise dedicated to Polybius from his banishment in Corsica. The tidings of great joy have changed the balance between human dejection and human elation.

but ἀεὶ δὲ χαίροντες, 2 Cor. vi. 10.   This almost excludes the meaning ' farewell.'

I will say] Not ' I say ' (A.V.).   In N.T., as in classical Greek, ἐρῶ is always future.

again] ' I am not forgetting the sorrow or the suffering ' : *c'est le sel de toutes nos joies.*

5. **your forbearing spirit**] Ἐπιεικής and ἐπιείκεια denote the " sweet reasonableness " which, by admitting limitations and making allowances, prevents *summum jus* from becoming *summa injuria.*   It forbears from insisting upon full rights, where rigidity would be harsh.   See Arist. *Eth. Nic.* V. x. 3.   In 2 Cor. x. 1 it is mentioned as a special characteristic of Christ.   ' Moderation ' (A.V.) and *modestia* (Vulg.) are too vague.   Acts xxiv. 4 we find ' clemency ' and *clementia*.   See Trench, § xliii.

become known to all men] Not merely to all Christians ; that they may admire it and imitate it ; Jn. xiii. 35.   For ἐγνώσθη cf. Lk. xxiv. 35 ; Acts ix. 24.

The Lord is at hand] Therefore be peaceful and patient ; 1 Cor. xvi. 22 ; Jas. v. 8 ; Heb. x. 24, 25 ; Rev. i. 7, iii. 11.* At any moment they may have to answer for their conduct ; and if any one is really wronged, his wrongs will be righted.   Retaliation here and now is altogether out of place.

The words might mean that ' the Lord is always near us,' and knows all that we think or do ; Clem. Rom. *Cor.* xxi. 3.   But that is not the probable meaning here, where the thought that the Lord will come soon suggests a warning against useless disquietude.

6. **needless anxieties**] Cf. 1 Cor. vii. 32.   ' Be careful for nothing ' (A.V.) is ambiguous and rather misleading. ' Never be full of cares ' might be better.   Μεριμνᾶν is ' to be full of cares which divide and distract the mind '; *curae quae meum animum divorse trahunt.*   Cf. Virg. *Aen.* iv. 285 f.   It is unreasonable anxiety, especially about things which we cannot control, not reasonable care about those which we can influence, that is here condemned ;

* See Murray's *Illustr. B.D.* art. ' Maranatha.'

see on ii. 20.   Jas. v. 13 gives the same remedy as is given
here for over-anxiety.   Cf. 1 Pet. v. 7.

in every case] Ἐν παντί, as in 1 Thess. v. 18.   While
πάντοτε marks limitless extension in time, ἐν παντί marks
limitless extension in sphere.   Vulg. has *in omni oratione et
obsecratione*, taking ἐν παντί with two feminine substantives.
Elsewhere it has *in omnibus* for ἐν παντί.   Prayer can
remove the feeling of helplessness ; *curare et orare plus inter
se pugnant quam aqua et ignis* (Bengel).

your prayer and your supplication] Both nouns have the
article, which may mean the prayer and the supplication
which is suitable, or which is usual in public worship.   See on
i. 4, and Trench, *Syn.* § li.

with thanksgiving] The duty comes naturally in an exhortation to joy.   For the combination with prayer see 1 Thess.
iii. 9, 10, v. 17, 18 ; Col. iv. 2 ; 1 Tim. ii. 1.   It was in the
stocks of the inner prison at Philippi that Paul and Silas
prayed and sang hymns to God ; Acts xvi. 25.

requests] Αἰτήματα, as in 1 Jn. v. 15.   A.V. has 'request.'
See Cremer, *Lex.* p. 73.

before God] Πρὸς τὸν Θεόν, *apud Deum*.   Cf. Jn. i. 1.
' Made known ' seems strange in such a connexion.   The
Psalms are full of such addresses to God.

7. **Then the peace**] ' Such will be a sure consequence
(καί) of casting all anxiety on the God who takes care of
you ' (1. Pet. v. 7).   It is the ' peace of God ' because He
bestows it ; and because He bestows it He is ' the God
of peace ' (*v.* 9 ; Rom. xv. 33 ; 1 Cor. xiv. 33).   It is the
atmosphere in which He exists, and which He desires to
communicate.   The peace is not dependent on the literal
granting of the requests.

will keep guard] A.V. has ' keep,' R.V. has ' guard.'   We
need both words to give the force of the military metaphor
in φρουρήσει.   Peace must always do sentry duty if its
rule is to be preserved from external and internal foes.
Most Latin authorities have *custodiat*, and some Greeks
comment as if we had an optative here.   The words are
a prophecy or a promise, not a prayer.

' Which passeth all understanding ' (A.V., R.V.), *i.e.* which
is beyond all power of comprehension, so that, as Augustine
says, not even Angels can understand it, makes excellent
sense ; but it is doubtful whether it is what the Apostle
means. He has been warning his converts against contentiousness and over-anxiety ; and he seems to mean that
God's peace produces far better results than human schem-
ing ; it is superior to all man's devices for security, and is
more efficacious in removing disquietude than any intellec-
tual effort or reasoning power. These often augment
disquietude. ' Surpasseth ' rather than ' passeth.'

your hearts and your minds] These two cover the spheres
in which dissensions and carking cares are generated.
Although νοήματα are commonly the *products* of νοῦς, and
therefore ' thoughts ' rather than ' minds,' yet here and 2
Cor. iii. 14, iv. 4, xi. 3 the thinking faculty seems to be
meant. See Hastings, *DCG.* and *DAC.* art. ' Heart.'   In
N.T. νόημα is exclusively Pauline.

in Christ Jesus] Not ' through ' (A.V.). The strong rock
and fortress (Ps. xxxi. 2, 3) in which Divine peace keeps
watch. What better security can Christian souls need ?

iv. 8, 9. EXHORTATION TO PRACTISE WHAT IS NOBLEST
AND BEST

'' Cherish beautiful thoughts. Live noble lives '' is Weymouth's summary. We have a generous encouragement
to the Philippians to take a broadminded view respecting
worthy ideals. There was much in their heathen views that
had to be absolutely abandoned ; but there was also much
that might be, and ought to be, valued and retained. Here
they needed knowledge and discernment (i. 9).

⁸ Finally, brethren, whatsoever things *are* true, whatsoever things
are honest, whatsoever things *are* just, whatsoever things *are* pure,
whatsoever things *are* lovely, whatsoever things *are* of good report :
if there be any virtue, and if there be any praise, think on these
things. ⁹ Those things which ye have both learned, and received,
and heard, and seen in me, do : and the God of peace shall be with
you.

" Nowhere has the born Jew approached so closely to
the moral ideal of the Greek philosophers as in the concep-
tions of honour and worth which he here strings together "
(Von Soden, *Early Christian Literature*, p. 113). " In
Phil. iv. 8 Paul himself, with full consciousness, includes
natural morality in Christian morality " (Clemen, *Primitive
Christianity*, p. 367).   See also Knowling, *Testimony of
St. Paul to Christ*, p. 491.

We have eight classes or points of view, which perhaps are
arranged in pairs : the last pair, by change of wording, is
separated from the rest.   The fifth and sixth classes are
also different from the first four.   They refer to men's
estimate of things, whereas the first four refer to realities,
without thought of estimates.   In paraphrasing it is
worth while to mark this grouping, which may be inten-
tional.

⁸ For the rest, Brethren, whatsoever things are really true, really
grand, really righteous, really pure, whatsoever things are lovely,
whatsoever things are winsome,—all the moral value that you were
wont to give to virtue and to the praise of mankind,—take these ideals
continually into account.   ⁹ Yet be not content with contemplating
ideals.   Go on and practise also the things which you learned and
received from me, and which you heard of me doing and saw me do.
Practise them in your daily lives.   Then the God who gives the
peace that you need will be with you.

8. **For the rest**] After the sudden and prolonged digression at iii. 1, the Apostle once more prepares to bring
the letter to a close.   The rendering of τὸ λοιπόν must be
the same in both places, implying that more remains to
be said.

really true] This and the following terms are to be understood in the widest and highest sense.   It is difficult to find
a good rendering for σεμνά.   A.V. gives ' honest,' with
' venerable ' in the margin ; R.V. ' honourable,' with
' reverend ' in the margin   ' Worthy,' ' dignified,' ' majestic,'
' august,' ' seemly,' ' wins respect ' are suggestions made by
translators and commentators.

lovely] Inspiring admiration and love ; *amabilia*, Vulg. ;

lieblich, Luther. Προσφιλής occurs nowhere else in N.T. In LXX ; Ecclus. iv. 7, xx. 13.

winsome] ' Of good report ' (A.V., R.V.) is not the meaning of εὔφημος : ' of gracious import ' would be nearer. Not ' well spoken of ' but ' well speaking,' *i.e.* expressing what is kind and likely to win people, and avoiding what is likely to give offence, is the meaning.

moral virtue] Nowhere else does St. Paul use ἀρετή, possibly because of its prominence in heathen philosophy. Here he uses it precisely because of that prominence. The Philippians' pagan ideas about intrinsic excellence were not wholly to be abandoned ; there was much that was noble in them and worthy of being remembered. In O.T. ἀρετή means ' glory ' or ' praise ' rather than ' virtue,' and hence perhaps the immediate mention of ' praise ' here. But in the Apocrypha the Greek philosophic meaning is frequent. See Hort on 1 Pet. ii. 9 ; Cremer, *Lex.* p. 646. Elsewhere in N.T., 2 Pet. i. 3, 5 only. In N.T. the Christian ideas of virtue are expressed by other terms ; δικαιοσύνη, ἁγιωσύνη, ἁγιότης, ἀγάπη, χρηστότης, εὐσέβεια, ἀγαθωσύνη.

praise of mankind] Whatever all men praise is sure to be worthy of consideration ; an Aristotelian principle. Cf. *securus judicat orbis terrarum.* See Hort on 1 Pet. i. 7 ; also Aug. *Ep.* ccxxxi. 4.

take into account] With a view to habitual conduct ; *horum rationem habete.* For λογίζεσθε see on iii. 13 ; the present imperative is here used of action which is to continue. Here we have the Apostle's " commendation of the Science of Ethics " (Beet).

9. **practice also]** Knowledge of what is noble without endeavour to realize it is fatal. In what follows we have two pairs, ' learned and received,' ' heard and saw,' and the two pairs are connected by ' and.' The καί which precedes the pairs (ἃ καί) is ' also,' not ' both ' (A.V., R.V.). The Philippians have two things to guide them ; the sum of what is noblest in human ideals, and the Apostolic teaching by word and example.

received] This is not a mere repetition of ' learned ' ;

παρελάβετε suggests that their teachers handed on to them
precepts which they themselves had been taught.   Cf.
I Thess. ii. 13, iv. 1 ; and Thess. iii. 6 ; 1 Cor. xvi. 1, 3.

heard of me doing] 'When I was absent from you.'   It
might mean ' heard me saying,' both clauses referring to his
presence.   Cf. i. 30 ; 2 Tim. i. 13, ii. 2.   St. Paul often
mentions himself, with or without his fellow-missionaries,
as a pattern for his converts to copy ; 1 Thess. i. 6 ; 2
Thess. iii. 7, 9 ; 1 Cor. iv. 16 ; Phil. iii. 17.   He explains why
he does so ; because, as the converts are well aware, he
himself endeavours to imitate Christ ; 1 Cor. xi. 1 ; Gal.
ii. 20.   To tell them to imitate Christ would in many cases be
less practical ; they had not yet had sufficient experience
of Christ.   A concrete example, set by those whom they had
seen and heard, would for a time be more effective.   *Vita
non minus quam ore virtutum dux fuerat ac magister* (Calvin).

Then] The καί is similar to that at the beginning of *v.* 7.
In both places the internal peace of the soul seems to be
specially meant.   Indirectly, by suppressing self-assertion,
this will promote peace in the Church.

the God of peace] Rom. xv. 33, xvi. 20.   See Westcott
on Heb. xiii. 20.   *Dieu est appelé le Dieu de paix : il fait
habiter dans sa maison ceux qui sont de même esprit et de
même cœur* (Bossuet).

iv. 10–20.   HISTORICAL AND PERSONAL

He once more returns from exhorting the Philippians to
the subject of himself ; and he here reaches the matter
which was one of the main reasons for sending the letter,
viz. the desire to express his gratitude for the gift which
they had sent to him.   He has already alluded to their
beneficence ; i. 5, 6, ii. 1, 12, 30 ; and the mention of the
' bishops and deacons ' at the outset may be prompted by
this same thought.   He now speaks definitely.

iv. 10–18.   GRATITUDE FOR THE PHILIPPIANS' GIFT.

[10] But I rejoiced in the Lord greatly, that now at the last your care of me had flourished again, wherein ye were also careful, but ye lacked opportunity.   [11] Not that I speak in respect of want : for I have learned in whatever state I am, therewith to be content. [12] I know both how to be abased, and I know how to abound : everywhere and in all things I am instructed, both to be full and to be hungry, both to abound and to suffer need.   [13] I can do all things through   Christ,   which   strengtheneth   me.   [14] Notwithstanding, ye have well done, that ye did communicate with my affliction. [15] Now ye Philippians know also, that in the beginning of the Gospel, when I departed from Macedonia, no Church communicated with me, as concerning giving and receiving, but ye only.   [16] For even in Thessalonica ye sent once and again unto my necessity.   [17] Not because I desire a gift : but I desire fruit that may abound to your account.   [18] But I have all and abound.   I am full, having received of Epaphroditus the things *which were sent* from you, an odour of a sweet smell, a sacrifice acceptable, wellpleasing to God.

These verses exhibit a characteristic combination of delicacy and independence. He is anxious to show that he is deeply touched and truly grateful, and also that his gratitude is not " a lively sense of future favours." His words have been criticized as wanting in proper feeling, and other estimates of them may be quoted. " The passage presents as tactful a treatment of a delicate matter as can well be found in the whole range of high literature " (Von Soden). " Courteous   expressions,   as   dignified   as they are delicate " (Meyer).   *Un modèle de bonne grace et de vive piété* (Renan).   " A singularly graceful and dignified postscript " (Barry).

[10] But I must not omit to say this.   It was a great joy to me in the Lord that already once more you revived in your thought for me : with a view to which you were really taking thought for me, but were lacking the opportunity of showing your solicitude.   [11] I do not mean that I was actually in want.   I was not ; for I for my part have learned in the circumstances in which I am to be content.   [12] I know also how to bear being reduced to penury ; I know also how to bear being in abundance.   In each and all circumstances of life I have been initiated into the secret of being able both to have plenty and to be famished, both to have abundance and to be in want.   [13] The secret is this : I have strength to bear everything when united with

Him who gives me such power. ¹⁴ Nevertheless, though I was not in great want, you did a noble thing in coming forward to have fellowship with me in my affliction by contributing to my support. ¹⁵ But you also yourselves, my Philippians, know well, without my reminding you, that this was no new thing with you ; because in the earliest days of the Gospel, when I departed from Macedonia, no Church had fellowship with me as regards giving and taking, with the sole exception of yourselves. In your case I allowed it. ¹⁶ Indeed I may say ' before I departed,' because even when I was still in Thessalonica you sent more than once to minister to my needs. ¹⁷ I repeat that I do not mean that I am desiring to have any gift from you. But I do mean that I am desiring that the fruit of your generosity should accumulate to your account in heaven. ¹⁸ And I can give a receipt in full for all that you owed me, and I have abundance over. I am fully supplied, seeing that I received from Epaphroditus the gifts which came from you.   They are an odour of a sweet smell, a sacrifice acceptable, well-pleasing to God.

10. **But I must not omit**] The δέ, as in 1 Cor. 16 and Gal. iv. 20, indicates that something has just occurred to him. He has been meaning to say it, but might have forgotten. The δέ looks back to 4–9, or perhaps earlier. ' I have been exhorting you to rejoice and to imitate me : so I must thank you for making me rejoice.'

great joy] Cf. Mt. ii. 10 ; Lk. ii. 10, xxiv. 52 ; Acts viii. 8, xv. 3. It is possible, with R.V., to regard ἐχάρην as an epistolary aorist ; ' it *is* a great joy.' In any case the verb is emphatic. See Augustine, *Confessions*, XIII. xxvi. 39 f.

in the Lord] It was a holy joy, not a mere casual emotion ; '' not of a worldly or ordinary kind '' (Chrys.).

already once more] Not νῦν, but ἤδη, which is made indefinite by the addition of πότε. See Sanday and Headlam on Rom. i. 10, the only other passage in N.T. in which the combination occurs.

revived] Like ' revived,' ἀνεθάλετε may be either active or neuter, ' revived your thought for me,' or ' revived in regard to your thought for me.' ' Budded forth again ' (Alford), ' shot forth afresh ' (Cunnington), *refloruistis pro me sentire* (Vulg.). Cf. Ecclus. i. 18, xi. 22, l. 10. To speak of ' reviving once more ' sounds somewhat like a complaint, an idea which he at once proceeds to dispel.

you were really] Imperfect, with καί for emphasis ; ' were really minding,' ἐφρονεῖτε, the favourite verb once more ; i. 7, ii. 2, etc. 'Εφ' ᾧ may mean ' seeing that,' or ' for which purpose.'

lacking the opportunity] A rare verb, ἀκαιρεῖσθαι, occurring here only in N.T. It is the opposite of εὐκαιρεῖν, 1 Cor. xvi. 12 ; Mk. vi. 31 ; Acts xvii. 21. It probably means that they had no one to send with their gift. Some understand ἀνεθάλετε of reviving *prosperity*, and ἠκαιρεῖσθε of lack of *means*.

11. **I do not mean**] Οὐχ ὅτι, as in *v.* 11 and iii. 12. This ellipse is a N.T. phrase. See on 2 Thess. iii. 9 ; 2 Cor. i. 24. In classical Greek it means ' not only,' or ' not but that.' Simcox, *Language of N.T.* p. 174 ; Blass, § 81, 1 ; Winer, p. 501. ' Not that I speak in respect of want ' (A.V., R.V.) is literal but not lucid. Lightfoot has ' in language dictated by want.' ' Want,' ὑστέρησις (here and Mk. xii. 44 only), implies actual penury.

I was not] This is implied in ἐγώ γάρ, ἐγώ is emphatic.

have learned] This is one of those cases in which it is the Greek idiom to use the aorist and the English to use the perfect. A. T. Robertson, *Gr.* p. 835. See on iii. 12.*

content] Independent of help and wealth, αὐτάρκης, Ecclus. xl. 18. M. and M., *Vocabulary*, p. 93. The less a man requires for himself, the more contented he is sure to be. See on 2 Cor. iii. 5, ix. 8 ; cf. 1 Tim. vi. 6. The richest man, said Socrates, is he who is content with least. *Beatus est praesentibus, qualiacunque sunt, contentus, amicusque rebus suis* (Seneca, *De Vita Beata*, vi. 2). *Se contentus est sapiens . . . egere enim necessitatis est ; nihil autem necesse sapienti est (Epist.* ix. 11, 12).

12. **reduced to penury**] As the great Example was. See on 2 Cor. viii. 9, xi. 7 ; cf. Phil. ii. 6, 7 ; Jas. i. 10.

in each and all] Ἐν παντὶ καὶ ἐν πᾶσιν, a vaguely com-

---

* Here again we seem to have rhetorically balanced clauses. ' I have learned ' balances ' I can do ' (*v.* 13), and between these statements we have four couplets in succession (*v.* 12). See J. Weiss in *Theologische Studien,* p. 191.

prehensive expression. Both παντί and πᾶσιν are neuter ; not
' in every circumstance and among all men.' Cf. 2 Cor. xi. 6.

been initiated] Μεμύημαι, one of a group of words which
the Apostle borrows from the language of pagan mysteries ;
e.g. μυστηριον, γνῶσις, νοῦς, σοφία, τελεῖος, and perhaps
πνεῦμα and ψυχή. R. M. Pope, *Intr. to Early Church
History*, pp. 43 f.

have plenty] Plenty of food, as both the word and the
context imply. In late Greek χορτάζεσθαι has quite lost
the notion of ' browsing.' It is used of human beings without
any suggestion that they are brutish in their food. Vulg.
satiari, Ambrstr. *saturari*. Cf. 1 Cor. iv. 11 ; 2 Cor. xi. 27.

have abundance and be in want] Once more (ii. 2, iii. 7–9)
the Apostle repeats without scruple in order to express his
meaning fully. He has just had ὑστέρησιν and περισσεύειν
and here he has περισσεύειν and ὑστερεῖσθαι. Cf. 1 Cor.
viii. 8 and 2 Cor. xi. 9.

13. **united with Him**] Lit. 'in Him '; cf. *vv.* 1, 7. 'Christ '
(A.V.) is an interpolation. In His strength, through union
with Him ; *in Christo, non propria virtute* (Calvin). The
statement is a paradox and a profound truth.* His dependence on Christ is the secret of his independence ; see on 2
Cor. xii. 9. Note the parallel couplets ; ' I have learned '
and so ' I know,' ' I have been initiated ' and so ' I have
strength.' For ἐνδυναμοῦν, ' to enable,' cf. 1 Tim. i. 12 ;
2 Tim. iv. 17.

14. **Nevertheless**] The uses of πλήν differ in this letter ;
i. 18, iii. 16, iv. 14. R.V. has ' Howbeit ' here, and elsewhere ' only.' Though his great joy was not caused by
relief from great want, yet it was real, because the relief
proved the generous sympathy of the Philippians.

did a noble thing] Mk. vii. 37 ; Acts x. 33. See Hort
on 1 Pet. ii. 12.

---

* *L'entreprise est grande ; mais le secours est égal au travail. Dieu,
qui vous appelle si haut, vous tend la main ; son Fils, qui lui est égal,
descend à vous pour vous porter. Dites donc avec Saint Paul : je puis
tout avec celui qui me fortifie* (Bossuet).
See also Cyril of Jerusalem, *Cat. Lect.* xxi. 4

fellowship with me in my affliction] ' To share it with me.'
" Co-operation is still the great demand among modern
Christians.   Churches so often leave it all for the pastor to
do." (A. T. Robertson, *Philippians*, p. 63.) For συνκοινωνεῖν
see Eph. v. 11 ; Rev. xviii. 4.   Cf. συνκοινωνός, i. 7 ; 1 Cor.
ix. 23 ; Rev. i. 9.   In these words the idea of personal
fellowship is prominent ; in μέτοχος and συνμέτοχος the
idea of participation in a common blessing.   Westcott
on Heb. iii. 1.   ' Communicate ' (A.V.) is now misleading ;
in 1611 it had the right meaning.

15. you also] ' As well as I.'

my Philippians] Very rarely does he address his converts
by name.   Here and 2 Cor. vi. 11 the passage is specially
affectionate.   Gal. iii. is hardly less so, in spite of the
epithet.   In all three places he brings his own life into
close connexion with that of his converts.*

in the earliest days] The beginning of the Mission to
Macedonia.

when I departed] If this means ' at the time of my departure,' there was some early contribution previous to what was
brought from Macedonia to Corinth.   See 2 Cor. xi. 9, where
the compound verb, προσανεπλήρωσεν, implies something *in addition*, and probably refers to previous gifts
of the Macedonians.   But ὅτε ἐξῆλθον may be a lax construction for ' when I *had* departed.'   Paley, *Horae Paulinae*,
VII. i. and iii.

as regards giving and taking] Perhaps we should say ' as
to the *account* of *credit* and *debit* ' ; *in ratione dati et accepti*,
Vulg.   In papyri λόγος occurs in the sense of ' account.'
See on *v.* 17 and cf. Ecclus. xli. 19, xlii. 7.   As in iii. 7, 8,
St. Paul may be adopting commercial language ; and if so,
his motive here may be to give a playful turn to a delicate
subject.†   Chrysostom interprets this as meaning that the
Philippians gave material gifts and received spiritual gifts.

* The form Φιλιππήσοι may come from *Philippenses*.   In secular
Greek we have Φιλιππεῖς and Φιλιππηνοί.

† That actual statements of accounts passed between the givers
and the receiver, as Zahn supposes, is very unlikely.

So also Pelagius, *dantes carnalia spiritualia accepistis.*
Theodore of Mopsuestia rightly rejects this. The meaning
is that what they gave he received. He worked for his
living, and accepted nothing from those among whom he
worked. In Thessalonica he accepted no support from
Thessalonians (1 Thess. ii. 9 ; 2 Thess. iii. 8) ; at Corinth
none from Corinthians (2 Cor. xi. 7, xii. 13) ; but in either
place he could accept gifts from Philippians.

16. **more than once**] Lit. ' both once and twice.' As in 1
Thess. ii. 18 ; Neh. xiii. 20 ; 1 Macc. iii. 30, the meaning
probably is ' twice.' This mode of numeration is Hebraic ;
Job. v. 19 ; Eccles. xi. 2 ; Amos i. 3, 6, 9, 11, 13, etc.

even when] Thessalonica was a larger and richer city
than Philippi.

to minister to] For this use of εἰς cf. i. 5 ; 2 Cor. ii. 12 ;
and see on 1 Cor. xvi. 1. M. and M. give illustrations,
Vocabulary, p. 186 *b*.

17. **I do not mean**] As in *v.* 11 and iii. 12.

I am desiring] As in ἐπιποθῶ (i. 8, ii. 26), the preposition
in ἐπιζητῶ is partly intensive, although it marks the direction of the desire rather than its intensity. As in *vv.* 1 and
12, repetition adds emphasis.

to your account] or ' to your credit ' ; *in rationem vestram,*
Vulg. Εἰς λόγον should probably have the same rendering
here and in *v.* 15. See on 2 Thess. i. 3.

18. **give a receipt in full**] This may be another commercial
metaphor. Papyri abundantly show that ἀπέχω was frequently used in this sense in the vernacular of the day.
Deissmann, *Bible Studies*, p. 229, *Light from Anc. East,*
pp. 110 f. ; M. and M., *Vocabulary*, p. 57. But the ordinary
meaning ' I have right out,' ' I have to the full ' (Mt. vi.
2, 5, 16 ; Lk. vi. 24) makes such excellent sense that it
may reasonably be adopted. In any case ἀπέχω forms
an antithesis to ἐπιζητῶ, ' so far from wanting I have
in full,' and we have repetition three words meaning
abundance.

odour of a sweet smell] A frequent expression in O.T.,
Gen. viii. 21 ; Exod. xxix. 18 ; Lev. i. 9 ; Ezek. xx. 41,

etc. Cf. 2 Cor. ii. 15 ; Eph. v. 2. The quotation helps the transition from the business aspect of the transaction to the religious one. There is " no justification for comparing the Persian idea, that the blessed dead would live among pleasant odours " (Clemen, *Primitive Christianity and its Non-Jewish Sources*, p. 171).

a sacrifice well-pleasing] As in Rom. xii. 1 ; Wisd. iv. 10. Cf. Heb. xiii. 16, and see Hort on 1 Pet. ii. 5. This does not mean that the gift had actually been offered at the altar. It means that it is the religious element in the gift that he specially values. Again we have repetition ; sweet smell, acceptable sacrifice, well-pleasing to God.

iv. 19, 20.   REQUITAL AND DOXOLOGY.

¹⁹ But my God shall supply all your need according to his riches in glory, by Christ Jesus. ²⁰ Now unto God and our Father *be* glory for ever and ever. Amen.

The Apostle can do no more than thank them, but he is sure that God will requite them.

¹⁹ You have pleased God by fully supplying all my needs, and God on my behalf will fully supply all your needs, according to the measure of the wealth which is His to bestow, not only here, but in the kingdom of glory, on those who are in Christ Jesus.
²⁰ Now to Him who is God and Father to us all be the glory which is due to Him for ever and ever. Amen.

19. **God on my behalf**] Such is the point of saying '*my* God ' here, *qui quod servo ejus datur remunerabitur* (Bengel). Cf. i. 3 ; Rom. i. 8 ; Philem. 4. ' And ' (R.V.) not ' but ' (A.V.) for δέ.

will fully supply] Fut. indic., not optat. as some Fathers read. Πληρώσει, ' will fill to the full,' as in *v*. 18. Cf. the futures in *vv*. 7 and 9.

all your needs] Every kind of need, material and spiritual.

according to the measure] ' On the scale of,' ' in accordance with.' Cf. Rom. xi. 33.

in the Kingdom of glory] 'Εν δόξῃ is added, lest any one should suppose that only earthly needs are meant, as

I

Theodore supposes. Theodoret limits the meaning to
τὸν ἐπουράνιον πλοῦτον, and no doubt heavenly riches
are specially meant ; but earthly benefits are not excluded.
The thought of this superabundant bounty coming from
God prompts an immediate doxology.*

20. **our God and father**] The change from ' my God '
to ' our God ' is natural. He is no longer thinking of God
acting on his behalf. Both here and Gal. i. 5 ' our ' belongs
to both ' God, and ' Father,' and in both places he would
wish to unite himself with his converts. See on 1 Thess. i. 3.

the glory] In the doxologies ' glory ' commonly has the
article, ἡ δόξα : Rom. xvi. 27 ; Gal. i. 5 ; Eph. iii. 21 ; 2 Tim.
iv. 18 ; Heb. xiii. 21 ; 1 Pet. iv. 11 ; 2 Pet. iii. 18.

for ever and ever] Lit. ' unto ages of ages,' a form peculiar
to N.T. and very frequent in the Apocalypse. Each ' age '
represents a long and indefinite period, and the whole
indicates an incalculable vastness of duration. Papyri
show how thoroughly Greek the prepositional combina-
tions with αἰών are. M. and M., p. 16.

iv. 21–23. CONCLUDING SALUTATIONS AND
BENEDICTION

[21] Salute every Saint in Christ Jesus : the brethren which are
with me greet you. [22] All the Saints salute you, chiefly they that are
of Caesar's household. [23] The grace of our Lord Jesus Christ *be*
with you all. Amen.

St. Paul very probably added this conclusion with his
own hand. See on 2 Thess. iii. 17.

[21] Greet in Christ Jesus every Christian in Philippi. All the brethren
who are my companions here send greetings to you. [22] All the
Christians in Rome send greetings to you, especially those who are
come from the Imperial household.
[23] The grace of the Lord Jesus Christ be with your spirit.

21. Greet in Christ Jesus] This is probably the true

---

* Bengel gives it a wider connexion : *Doxologia fluit ex gaudio
totius epistolae*. But cf. Rom. xi. 36 ; Gal. i. 5.

connexion. See Robertson and Plummer on 1 Cor. xvi. 19, where ἐν κυρίῳ must be taken with ἀσπάζεται, and cf. Rom. xvi. 22. But 'every saint in Christ Jesus ' may be right ; cf. Rom. xvi. 11, 12, 13. Papyri supply abundant evidence that ἀσπάζομαι was the regular word for expressing greetings at the close of a letter. M. and M., p. 85.

every Christian] Of whatever kind. See on i. 1. We need not, with Theodore, exclude nominal Christians. Even they have been consecrated.

my companions here] The companions who visited him most frequently in his imprisonment, especially Timothy.

22. All the Christians] Even those who are censured in ii. 20, 21. We must have either ' greet ' or ' salute ' in all three places ; not ' salute,' ' greet,' ' salute.'

the Imperial household] The *domus Caesaris* or *familia Caesaris*, which would include every one from high officials down to slaves. Such persons might have the privilege of visiting those who were in prison, at any rate such as had appealed to Caesar. That Seneca was one of these is a baseless conjecture. As Philippi was a Roman colony, with a number of veteran soldiers among its population, this greeting from Caesar's household would be much appreciated. In any case it is noteworthy that the Gospel *in illum scelerum omnium et flagitiorum abyssum penetravit* (Calvin). There is little doubt that Christianity had entered the Imperial household before St. Paul reached Rome. There were many Jews among the lower officials in Nero's household, and it was perhaps among them that the Gospel made its first converts. See Lightfoot, *Biblical Essays*, pp. 321 f. ; Sanday and Headlam, *Romans*, pp. xviii. f. ; Ramsay, *Paul the Traveller*, p. 353 ; and the references in Renan, *L'Antechrist*, pp. 11-13.

23. The grace of the Lord] The common form of the Apostle's final Benediction, τὴν συνήθη εὐλογίαν (Theodoret), which, however, varies somewhat in details. See on 1 Thess. iv. 28 and 2 Thess. iii. 18. The ordinary secular conclusion was ' Fare ye well,' ἔρρωσθε, Acts xv. 29, or ' Farewell,' ἔρρωσο. Cf. 3 Jn. 2.

with your spirit] This is the true reading. A.V. follows inferior authorities, which have μετὰ πάντων for μετὰ τοῦ πνεύματος. 'With your spirit' occurs Gal. vi. 18 and Philem. 25; 'with thy spirit' 2 Tim. iv. 22. We might expect 'with your spirits': but the generic singular is usual; 1 Thess. v. 23; Rom. viii. 16; cf. Rom. vi. 12; 1 Cor. vi. 19.

The 'Amen,' as usual, is an addition borrowed from the liturgies; but in Gal. vi. 18 and Jude 25 it may be original.

Indexes

INDEX I. GENERAL

Abbott, E. A., 34, 53, 58
Advent, Second, 11, 16, 84, 86
Alford, xxii, 100
Alternations in the Epistle, xvii, xviii, 17, 33, 55
Ambrosiaster, xxi, 68
Amen, 108
Antinomianism condemned, 76
Aorist, Force of the, 19, 28, 45, 54, 62, 77
Epistolary, 60, 62, 100
Sometimes = English perfect, 50, 77, 101
Apostle, 1, 61
Appian, vii
Aristotle, 39, 93
Article, Absence of the, 4, 54, 65, 72, 84
Force of the, 12, 21, 23, 26, 29, 31, 39, 48, 58, 61, 63, 68, 73, 74, 75, 85, 106
Attraction of the pronoun, 35
Augustine, 12, 24, 52, 95, 97, 100
Authenticity of the Epistle, xi, xii
A.V., Defects in the, 8, 19, 23, 31, 35, 39, 47, 52, 53, 57, 59, 61, 72, 81, 84, 95, 97

Bacon, B. W., xiii
Barry, A., xxii, 35, 99
Baur, F. C., xi
Beet, J. A., xxii, 50, 65, 66, 97
" Belly," Meaning of word, 83
Benediction, Concluding, 107
Bengel, xii, xxii, 9, 10, 13, 14, 24, 25, 28, 30, 35, 45, 48, 51, 58, 59, 61, 76, 88, 94, 105, 106
Benjamin, Tribe of, 71
Bernard, J. H., 42
Beza, 4, 23, 25, 42, 53, 57, 61, 62, 73, 74
Blass, vii, 21, 29, 30, 52, 73, 75, 85, 101
Bleek, xi, xii

Bondservant, 2, 45
Book of Life, 91
Bossuet, 12, 13, 42, 52, 98
Bourdaloue, 51, 52, 86
Brethren, 19, 65, 78
Briggs, C. A., 6, 42
Bruce, A. B., xxiii
Burrhus, xv
Burton, E. de Witt, 15, 26, 30, 36, 38, 60, 70, 75, 80

Caesar's Household, xiv, 107
Caesarea, Imprisonment at, xiii, 20, 59
Calvin, xxi, 14, 21, 23, 29, 31, 53, 57, 72, 80, 81, 86, 98, 102, 107
Case, S. J., 6, 16, 48, 75
Cassiodorus, 4
Change of tense, 19, 28
Characteristics of the Epistle, xvi–xviii, 9, 37, 65
Charles, R. H., 5, 91
Chiasmus, 23, 74
Christ Jesus, 3, 11
Christology, 6, 40–49
Chrysostom, xxi, 23, 24, 37, 49, 57, 62, 65, 69, 71, 90, 92, 100, 103
Cicero, 47
Circumcision, the true and the worthless, 69
Clemen, xii, 96, 105
Clement of Alexandria, 90
Clement of Philippi, 91
Clement of Rome, xii, 5, 30, 33, 79, 93
Climax, 45, 71
Coming, Second, 11, 16, 84, 86
Commentaries, xxi
Comparatives strengthened, 30
Compounds, 26, 27, 46, 51, 64, 84
Double, 76, 79, 84
with σύν, 11
with ὑπέρ, 48

Printed in Great Britain for ROBERT SCOTT Publisher, PATERNOSTER ROW, LONDON, E.C., by BUTLER & TANNER FROME AND LONDON

evangelical masterworks

Unsurpassed quality from top scholars and theologians

A COMMENTARY ON ST. PAUL'S EPISTLE
TO THE PHILIPPIANS
by Alfred Plummer
Insight into Paul's letter of joy, with particular reference to the original language.

COMMENTARY ON THE EPISTLE
TO THE EPHESIANS
by Charles Hodge
A skillful exposition of the epistle's practical instructions and doctrinal positions.

THE DIRECTORY OF THE DEVOUT LIFE
by F. B. Meyer
An inspiring collection of meditations on the Sermon on the Mount.

GREAT CHAPTERS OF THE BIBLE
by G. Campbell Morgan
The renowned Bible teacher analyzes favorite chapters from the Old and New Testaments.

HOLINESS
by John Charles Ryle
A masterful discussion of the Christian's objective—to become more like Jesus.

NOTES ON THE MIRACLES OF OUR LORD
by Richard C. Trench
A comprehensive work on an important phase of our Lord's ministry: miracles.

NOTES ON THE PARABLES OF OUR LORD
by Richard C. Trench
The Bible scholar offers insights into our Lord's manner of teaching by parables.

PROGRESS OF DOGMA
by James Orr
A discussion of how the various doctrines in the church's theology have developed.

ST. PAUL'S EPISTLES
TO THE THESSALONIANS
by George Milligan
A verse-by-verse examination of the Greek text with special background material about the first-century church.

THE TREASURY OF SCRIPTURE
KNOWLEDGE
Introduction by R. A. Torrey
Thousands of biblical passages are explained through the application of other Scripture passages.